SHIP
TAVERN.

THE HIDDEN NAVY

THE HIDDEN NAVY

EVELYN BERCKMAN

HAMISH HAMILTON
LONDON

First published in Great Britain, 1973
by Hamish Hamilton Ltd.
90 Great Russell Street, London, W.C.1.

Copyright © 1973 Evelyn Berckman

SBN 241 02352 1

Printed in Great Britain by
T. & A. Constable Ltd., Edinburgh

To

H.M.'s

R.N.

Past, present and future

CONTENTS

ILLUSTRATIONS

Between pages 34 and 35

ACKNOWLEDGMENTS

I HAVE to thank Lieutenant-Commander P. K. Kemp, Naval historian, antiquarian and Admiralty Archivist (retd) for unwearied help and encouragement, given with royal generosity over a period of many years.

To Mr E. K. Timings, Principal Assistant Keeper of the Public Record Office, I offer my profound gratitude for his interest and invaluable guidance. Also I thank Mr Norman Evans, Assistant Keeper of the PRO, as much for his unfailing assistance as for his comforting accessibility on occasions of need.

For the jacket design of the Fouled Anchor I am indebted to Mr Bailey and Miss Riley of the Admiralty Library, by whose kind assistance is reproduced this superb seal and symbol, as well as the likeness of John Nicol.

For the illustrations and endpapers I am indebted to the following, all of the National Maritime Museum: Mr B. T. Carter, Head of the Department of Paintings and Prints; Mr Archibald, Deputy Head; Mrs Tucker, Research Assistant; Miss Elizabeth Myhill of the same Department; Mr Waite, a Principal Officer of Ships; Mr Peter Ince, Research Assistant of the Department of Navigational Instruments, from all of whom I have received enlightenment, accomplished instruction, and the most charming kindness.

I am grateful to Miss Dorothy Stroud, Assistant Keeper of Sir John Soane's Museum, for drawing the Mudge Chronometer to my attention, and for her singularly gracious cooperation in having it photographed. The Parker Gallery of Bond Street gave generous permission to photograph the rare Stothard print, and I am indebted to Mr Michael Robinson, sometime Head of Paintings at the National Maritime, for informing me of its whereabouts. Finally I have to thank Mr Michael Ross-Wills and his assistant, Mr Perks, for the photographs, and for the expert and painstaking care that made their quality possible.

To all the foregoing I offer, above all, my sense of great good fortune in meeting persons whose knowledge and attainments enable them to smooth the researcher's path and to place at his service so varied—and so eminent—a quality of help.

*

The chapter on the waterfront and stowaway prostitute except, the entire book is drawn from consecutive readings of the State Papers Domestic between 1580 and 1860. The chapter on the women, since their existence was denied or suppressed by absence of allusion in all official records except on rare and un-avoidable occasions, is drawn from the State Papers Domestic whenever possible, but has had to be supplemented from Admiralty Regulations; also from contemporary pamphlets, whose titles and authorship are indicated in the text.

A bibliography has been avoided, and all numbered references appear in footnotes, where reference to the Papers is abbreviated as SPD.

THE FLOATING RIB

CAMP follower, a term anciently and dishonourably imbedded in the language, over recent years has been so far reduced in impact as to convey a derogation half-jocular and more often political than not. Yet the word in its original and literal sense paints, on receding canvases of the past, an image eternally changeless and eternally ruinous in outline and colouring. Where marching armies left their multitudinous trail of bare heels or sandals or military boots, in that same dust was set the footprint of the rear-guard who came limping after in all its lamentable panoply of rags and shredding ribbons, verminous curls and variegated infection.

Yet side by side with this timeless story imprinted on the marching spoor runs an identical one, written not in dust but in water; acted out not on land but in the foul obscurities and lower-deck darkness of ten thousand thousand ships. Just as it may be supposed that the institution of camp follower is as old as the earliest existing armies, so it is reasonable to conjecture that the stowaway whore or seaport whore is as old as the traffic of the seas. From history's dawn the ocean has been restless with the sails of every race and every occupation, plus the marauders who preyed on them and the fleets for convoy, defence or attack. By legend, allusion and tradition first and written evidence later, it is plain in how many such ships there would be women aboard; covertly or openly, depending on the rank of their protectors or the laxness of superintendence when the ship lay in port. Especially prior to conceptions of injury to health or discipline, the presence of the high-grade or low-grade female passenger was openly

allowed or winked at. As early as 1587 the printed regulations of
the Armada, with their explicit prohibition of women aboard,
and promise of *severe punishment* for contravening the order
regardless of the offender's rank, testify how entrenched the
custom was, how ancient and taken for granted.

The presence of concealed women in Naval ships has the
insubstantial quality of a haunting—something rumoured but
largely unseen. Increasingly regulated out of existence as centuries
advanced, all the same these shadows were so often smoked from
their holes by accident, disaster or emergency, that their fleeting
yet constant appearances seem to suggest a whole unsuspected
dimension, on the same principle that one rat, seen daily on a
farm, guarantees a population of at least twenty. But the glimpses
we catch of this creature—the living ones, that is—are usually in
snatches, or combined with unpredictable circumstance; and
even from these she retreats again, quickly, into the lower-deck
shadow.

Formal or consecutive records of the humblest class of whore
afloat—the true stowaway, boring her channel from dark hold
to dark hold, as ship after ship was anchored or paid off—may
be stated, without qualification, not to exist. Far from getting into
commanders' routine reports or correspondences, the topic was a
universal matter of retreat rather than approach, of the blind eye,
the wide detour and similar dodges of avoidance. Leaving the
fifteenth century and approaching the sixteenth, when Naval
reports became more and more highly organized, there is equal
scarcity of *direct* allusion. Only in the seventeenth century, when
the practice was flourishing with the pestilential abandon of a
vermin colony, does the very occasional voice protest—not
officially but privately, and for all the notice taken of it might
have spared itself the effort. Only in the eighteenth century—
when among the better-educated ideas of morality, hygiene and
discipline had begun to crystallize as we know them, or used to—
do we find explicit objections and unsparing descriptions, *in print*.
Not that, again, of regular and periodic Naval issues, but of
pamphlets privately printed and paid for out of the authors' own
pockets.

Accordingly, in State archives of commanders' and others' correspondences preserved by the hundred thousand, mention of the watery footprint is rare or negligent enough to communicate nothing, virtually, of its measure. Only by way of flotsam and jetsam does it come to the surface; only by way of hints widely scattered, infrequent writings surviving by luck or accident; a lost, drowned story. And matching this submerged quality, the stowaway prostitute can claim her unique and submerged distinction: that where the army straggler has her title of camp follower, her sea-going sister secretly in the ship's hold is still more secret in not even possessing, by way of identity, any name of her own.

A clear distinction must be made between the prostitute illicitly *living* aboard ship, and the visiting prostitute, a shore-dwelling class whose characteristics will be attempted later. Again, among the prostitutes actually in residence in the ship, a second distinction must be made between the highest class—the ranking officers' women—and the lowest, the destitute creature secretly harbouring in the common seamen's hold. Both classes, in point of illegality, were equal. But where the admiral's or captain's mistress paraded the upper deck, secure under protection more or less powerful according to rank, the seaman's doxy maintained her shadowy tenure only by never being seen at all.

It is the pursuit of this phantom of the lower depths which is the most defeating of any, presenting as she does a phenomenon common to phantoms but unique among sea-going populations —of invisibility in a literal sense, or very nearly literal. Constantly she repels every effort at forcing her to materialize as a person, or to concede—in some rare and fleeting appearance—any individual or characteristic quality. She is a creature of hearsay, of oldest tradition, unhonoured by any reference of ribaldry or sea-chanty. Furtiveness was her passport, cunning her ticket into the ship's bowels, a highly developed avoidance of observation her guarantee of permanency in darkness. The preamble of her first entrance into the ship was probably one of lurking in the dockside uproar and confusion, her eye never leaving the overworked first lieutenant in charge of taking on supplies, and whose attention could not be in ten places at once; snatching her chance for a lightning swoop down a hatchway, to be met—this seems essential—by the man or men who were her sponsors. Then, in whatever dark crack of concealment they had found for her, she endured voyages of weeks and months, kept alive on whatever the seamen could spare her from their own rations of rotten meat and biscuit and scummed water; or by the greatest good luck that could happen to her (one might suppose), not surviving at all. Yet improbably by her own viva voce testimony—when we have caught up with it—this creature of a thousand horrible endurances preferred to go on living.

None of all this, once more, derives from the one incontrovertible witness, the woman herself. Where is she, this first-hand, material witness? Where and how can she be compelled to assume a form and a voice of her own, available to our eyes and hearing? Centuries will pass before a solitary specimen is captured and held in the beam of faint light which is partly her own faint voice, partly the voices of her intimate associates. Till then this blurred presence—so victimized and defenceless, yet rightly recognized from earliest times as dangerous and sinister—existed only by reference more or less oblique, in which one specific detail may be sought in vain.

Allusions

When the Armada was preparing to invade England her commander, the Duke of Medina Sidonia, included in his orders a sharp and specific one: *No public women aboard the ships.* This was in 1588. About ten years later a great man now middle-aged and a prisoner in the Tower, Sir Walter Raleigh, was trying to help a young friend whom he loved and who loved him: Prince Henry, elder son of James I. An alarmingly brilliant boy, he had neatly summed up both King and captive in the words, 'Who but my father would keep such a bird in a cage!' and, in his own person, illustrated the tradition that the best often die young. At the moment, however, he was not only alive but more alive than usual, since a line-of-battle ship was to be built under his direct sponsorship and supervision; though only thirteen he was engrossed in the sciences of warfare and went passionately at any problem concerning them.

Raleigh well understood how thrilled Henry was and, equally thrilled, put his great experience as a seaman at his Prince's disposal in the form of notes entitled, *Excellent Observations Concerning the Royall Navy*. Every word of it is fascinating, down to his homely concern that a kettle should always be kept boiling in the kitchen, as it was called at the time. Among his more major considerations of construction, speed and so forth, he specified a certain practice of contemporary ship-building that he hated and would like to abolish, which was the custom of making a number of little shelters or 'cabbins' on the upper deck. One cabin for the Master was quite enough, he stated, and went on to explain his condemnation of additional ones: *Albeit the Marriners doe covet store of Cabbins, yet indeed they are but sluttish Dens that breed sicknesse, serving to cover stealths.*

The implication seems unmistakable, yet 'sluttish' in Raleigh's mouth is not so indicative as one might think; the word in the language of his day did not convey (as to us) a connotation exclusively female. It is difficult, however, to envisage what 'stealths' breed 'sicknesse', except the obvious ones. Perhaps Raleigh meant this, perhaps not; or perhaps he stated the case obliquely, out of deference to Henry's youth. But if the absolute significance of his words is debatable, there is no debating the fact of Medina Sidonia's directive against the practice, nor the depth of its roots and rankness of its growth implied by his stringency of prohibition.

Raleigh died on the scaffold, to the eternal infamy of James I who sent him there in 1618, and fifteen years later an unattractive baby (to judge by his maturer portraits) was born in London. But the baby had abilities of the highest and became an early example, if not the earliest, of the really first-class, thoroughly professional Naval administrator: Samuel Pepys. One of his closest friends was James Houblon, a wealthy merchant whose business took him to various foreign ports, and on May 7, 1677 Houblon sent him a letter—a letter remarkable for putting into words the thing that everyone knew, and considered hardly worth comment, or even a thought. A certain hesitancy in his appeal might be conjectured, since he realized that Pepys must know more about it than he could ever know. Yet all the same something specially flagrant—some particular violation of his sense of decency—drove him into imploring Pepys 'that the King's ships may not be made Baudy houses nor the Captains publiquely carry and entertain their whores on board—and that from port to port in the Mediterranean, to the Great scandall of turks Jews and Christians'.

Extraordinary as this letter is in having been written at all, it is still more extraordinary in never having been answered. Pepys conducted an enormous correspondence on every branch of Naval affairs, of which every single letter was duplicated in beautifully written ledgers. The most casual look at any such ledger also reveals his promptness in answering all communications. Then how could he receive a complaint so radically serious, and be silent? The answer must be that he wrote privately, or waited till he could answer Houblon verbally. But perhaps even his silence says this much: that such a topic must not appear in his records; not because he feared its mention (since he kept Houblon's letter) but for other reasons. Perhaps this scandal was like the perennial dockyards scandal—something that everyone knew and no one wanted to touch. Bringing up officially at the Navy Board what had never gained official cognizance was as sure of defeat as prejudicial to his own career.

Other personal and professional considerations might deter him. His ledgers reveal that the King himself attended most of the business meetings at the Navy Office; was Charles II the man to impose monastic regimes on his sailors? And no more did Pepys desire to explore means of safeguarding the seaman's virtue; he was no fonder of looking a fool than anyone else. But any cherisher of the past must dally with the thought that his answer to Houblon (if he did answer in writing) may still be hidden in some forgotten box of old papers, waiting for a lucky discoverer.

Only sixteen years after Houblon's letter another protest was registered (October 5, 1693) and this one is remarkable not only for its outspokenness, but in being addressed to the fountain of authority, the King himself. The writer this time was a Mr Richard Gibson; though only a clerk in the Navy Office, his handling of Naval business in general must have given him a wide view of many problems, and what Raleigh may have hinted at ninety-three years before comes out boldly and unequivocally in his statement:

'Your Maties petitioner humbly represents, that all manner of debauchery, to a scandal, is too common in your Navy; *which proves the parent of great sickness and mortality*; occasioning thousands of your seamen to do you little service, by their going ashoar for a cure.'

If the scandalized merchant's protest on moral grounds and the mere look of the thing were valid enough, how much more valid is Gibson's, with its unsparing conjunction of the seaman's prostitute with disease and the inevitable sequels of disease: physical deterioration and lowered efficiency.

Nevertheless, in spite of this new explicitness, the slow-grinding mills of God had stiff competition from the slower-grinding mills of Admiralty. Not for another thirty-seven years do any regular Naval directives seem to exist in printed form except for edicts and proclamations issued in emergency. But in January, 1731, there appears a printed book entitled: REGULATIONS AND INSTRUCTIONS RELATING TO HIS MAJESTIES SERVICE AT SEA, ESTABLISHED BY HIS MAJESTY IN COUNCIL. With great minuteness the book details the duties of every officer and warrant officer, dividing and subdividing each department of the ship. And here, under *Instructions to the Captain*—after hundreds of years—we find for the first time an *official* admission of what was tacitly but comprehensively barred from official mention: *He is not to carry any Woman to Sea . . . without Orders from the Admiralty*. But the regulation is so perfunctory and undetailed that authority seems to brush past it as hastily as possible—especially since the men who framed it fail entirely to give it a definite grade in the scale of offences. Still less do they apply a specific punishment for the specific violation, such as the wooden collar prescribed for *Swearing, Cursing, or Blaspheming the Name of God*. It is true that further along, under the section headed THE MASTER-AT-ARMS, we find: *He is to acquaint the Officer of the Watch with all Misdemeanours and Irregularities committed in the Ship, which shall come to his Knowledge.* But again the Irregularities are not defined, and if these by tradition are mostly Fighting and Smoking, description never comes down squarely on other offences.

No new book of Regulations came out till 1734. This edition repeats the loose and ungeneralized order to captains, *He is not to carry any woman to sea.* But later in the same issue, again we find something more specific in terms of allusion, if nothing stronger. *The Commanders are strictly required to be very vigilant to suppress all dissolute, immoral and disorderly practices.*

'Dissolute and Immoral' seem (by individual guess only) rather too mild to apply to the homosexual, always referred to with ferocious hatred and loathing, and for whom the punishment was as drastic as final. If, therefore, *dissolute and immoral* are to the nearest available address, the next *Captains' Instruction* is not without humour—seeing that the woman stowaway's presence would be known to the entire lower deck: *He is to correct those who are guilty of the same.* 'Correct': experienced commanders must have surveyed the word with sardonic eyes. Were they to rebuke the man privately? publicly? apply the same punishment as for Swearing and Cursing? The wooden collar might be seen as inappropriately sited for the activity it was supposed to put down, and in any case there would hardly be enough collars to go around. As for invoking the penalty of flogging 'for men who were guilty of the same', the problem would be to find one man whose innocence of 'the same' qualified him to swing the cat.

The nocturnal chaperon of the seaman was, as mentioned earlier, the Master-at-Arms. Continuous from 1731 to 1745 are his instructions to 'acquaint the Officer of the Watch with all Irregularities'; and with the repetition of this directive in all editions, the extent of his power becomes evident. On him depended considerably the climate of the men's lives. If in making

his rounds he observed a reasonable latitude or moderate indulgence according to circumstances, existence might be tolerable;
if on the other hand he had an appetite for the exercise of petty
authority and the infliction of small tyrannies, or actively enjoyed
bullying, tale-bearing or cruelty, the seaman could look forward
to a guaranteed hell of constricting observances and savage
penalties. If he were dishonest, bribes to turn the blind eye might
enter the picture; if he were honest, all the same his own compassion or sense of futility might work on him to the point of
unwilling condonations; if he had common sense, he might be
influenced by the risk of being attacked by the men he interfered
with, and—physical risk aside—by the possibility that in such
repeated incidents might lie the germ of large-scale mutiny.

No memoirs of Masters-at-Arms exist to prove or disprove this
view. But that his surveillance was found less than ideally effective
seems all but proven by the edition of 1746, which transfers his
duties to a higher officer, a lieutenant (rank not specified; there
were six grades). This unfortunate lieutenant is now the recipient
of instructions: *In the Night he is to visit the Ship between Decks,
to see that there be no Disorder among the Men.* This remains unchanged between 1745-55, while the inadequate *He shall carry no
Woman to Sea* bleats on as usual.

All at once, in 1756, the Captains' Instructions are hotted up,
with a particularity of language hitherto non-existent:

ADDITIONAL REGULATIONS

*That no Woman ever be permitted on Board, but such as are really
the Wives of the Men they come to, and the Ship not to be too much
pestered even with them. But the Indulgence is only tolerated while the
Ship is in Port, and not under Sailing Orders.*

At last authority was genuinely coming to grips with the
problem, or trying to; in this latest directive we see its latest
bright idea, lawful matrimony applied as a yardstick. How well
this pathetic device stood up in the end may be demonstrated by
looking thirty years ahead and seeing how its restrictions, taken
one by one, worked out:

1756 (Directive)
No Women in the Ship, but such as are really the Men's Wives.

1797
'Women ... and their reputed husbands ... still infest H.M.'s
Ships in great numbers.'

1756 (Directive)
*The Indulgence is only tolerated while the Ship is in port, and not
under Sailing Orders.*

1797
Women classified as wives, whether the genuine or spurious
article, not only sailed in first-rates on combat duty, but did men's
work during large-scale sea-engagements, including those major
ones with Napoleon's fleet; of the very humble-class women who
applied for medals after the Battle of the Nile as having made up
the teams of five necessary to serve each muzzle-loader, all were
aboard first-rates. Moreover St Vincent, in his 1797 complaint
on female infestation, included another and specially lethal one:
'The leakage and waste of water [is caused by] the Women'.

Yet for all that bitter capitalized Women it will be noticed that,
inflamed as he is over the loss of the precious water, even this
greatest of all seamen and *constructive* disciplinarians offers no
direct prohibition, nor even suggestion of one. St Vincent's
harshness, like that of every eminent Naval commander, was
tempered by a sort of unsentimental compassion and a profound
awareness of the limits of human endurance, and indeed the
common seaman of the eighteenth century—heaving with new
volcanic resentments and new articulateness against injustice, yet
still kept in control by an ancient vigilant brutality—was a force
better not driven to exploding point. But the great Admiral's
failure to take really stringent measures of any kind proves, as
hardly anything does, what those standing *Regulations on Women*
amounted to.

From 1757 to 1805 there are no new rules concerning women:
year after year *He is not to carry any Woman to Sea* confronts us.

But all at once in 1806—after seventy-five years of the tired old formula—the ruling is dropped from the Captains' Instructions. Instead we find—perhaps significantly—that the Lieutenant no longer goes the nightly rounds. The Master-at-Arms has resumed this office, but with a difference; he is now directly responsible to the Lieutenant, and the Lieutenant is directly responsible for seeing that he performs his duties with great strictness. The chief emphasis has shifted elsewhere: 'He shall go his rounds every half hour to see that no candles or lamps are burning, or men smoking.' The fear of fire, ever present—and another fear: 'The Gunner must examine the lashings of the guns once in each watch.' The havoc of a five-ton cannon on wheels, broken loose in a rolling sea, is inferior only to the havoc of fire in a wooden ship full of ammunition, and brings home some of the environments of the lower-deck men—and women.

By 1808, mysteriously, reappears the incantation, *He shall not carry any woman to sea.* Simultaneously we note that the nightly patrol is reinforced; now the Lieutenant in person must head the Master's half-hourly inspection among all those freighted hammocks. In this constant rearranging and stiffening of the surveillance, custodians set to watch custodians, first the Master, then the Lieutenant, then the first reporting to the second, then the second accompanying the first—we perceive authority perennially trying to cope with the problem, and perennially defeated.

The three editions of 1813 Regulations, and one of 1815, were unchanged. All at once, however, the issue of 1824 grips with the cold, tightening exactness of modernity:

ARTICLE 15: *He is not to allow the wife of any Officer to be carried to sea in the Ship, without the previous permission, in each case, of the Lords Commissioners of the Admiralty,* NOR ANY OTHER WOMAN, *without such permission.*

'Nor any other woman' gives the game away; the extra proviso would not exist if the condition did not also exist, or rather survive.

In 1826 and 1833 the Master-at-Arms is no longer required to go on his nightly prowl every half-hour. As civilization creeps in the seaman's tattered Polly seems to recede—but not to vanishing point, not yet. In 1844 a printed form called *The State and Condition of H.M.'s Ship*   on   *Station*, gives a full and detailed list of persons aboard a certain ship, and included in this list is the curious entry, *Smuggles*. This is the first hint of official written acknowledgment, during 111 years, that unlicensed persons may be aboard. The sex of 'Smuggles' is discreetly withheld, but the very discretion may be significant. Included in the same 1844 Regulations is another form, *Passing Certificate for a Surgeon*, which quaintly specifies that he shall be proficient in Midwifery. Inappropriate skill to demand of a warship's doctor, but indubitably necessary for those legitimate female passengers who were officers' wives, from the captain downward, and no less necessary—it may be—for the poor stowaway stricken with labour in the fetid hold, whose cries and groans, not to be muffled, gave away the secret of her presence.

Direct Evidence

On an April day of 1636 the Naval Commissioners sent Phineas Pett, master ship-builder at Chatham, to direct salvage efforts where the *Anne Royal* was lying on her side in the mud, with part of her keel broken off through coming violently aground. Pitt's despondent report on the unlikelihood of getting 'such a bulk of waight' upright again, and on the charges which are already staggering, has included: 'Divers men drowned, and *some women*.'

In this and other instances, the most frequent confirmation of the woman secretly aboard is the discovery of her dead body. Yet extraordinary emergencies sometimes cause—or even compel —this phantom to materialize, to the simulated or genuine astonishment of upper-deck eyes.

In May, 1815, the *Horatio* struck on a needle rock, and the sea came flooding in at the rate of eight inches a minute. All hands were turned to the pumps; after a quarter-hour of frantic exertions an attempt was made to build up a rim of water-resistant oakum around the gash, press a sail down over it, and seal its edges with more oakum. This process was called *thrumming*. But thrumming on this scale took time and sufficient helpers, all hands were needed at the pumps, and the situation was of desperate extremity.

All at once five women appeared on the scene. Only one of them was known to the officer relating the episode; she was the boatswain's wife. By his manner of reference to the others he had never set eyes on any of them, which points to the reasonable inference that they were stowaways. Quickly they took over at the lethal break, releasing the men who were needed at the pumps, and 'rendered essential service in thrumming the sail'. The moment they succeeded in sticking it down firmly, 'a change was felt at the pumps', says the narrator, and one hears the great breath of relief. The rate of pumping, a singularly terrible exertion, is specified in Admiralty papers: 500 to 800 strokes a minute for serious emergency, or eight to twelve strokes a second respectively. The ship being saved, the four unknown apparitions melted away again into their secret holes.

Yet, if only to one person, and by implication rather than relation, the narrative seems infinitely moving. The lieutenant knew nothing, or seemed to know nothing, of the four stow-aways; the boatswain's wife, on the other hand, must have known all about them. How otherwise could she have recruited her working team from the hold as quickly as she did? But her knowledge she had kept to herself, till faced by the threat of the ship's going down with all hands. Was her earlier silence through mere silent partisanship of sex? through obscure compassion for those fallen into the nethermost pit, whose lot she would not make harder by betrayal? Had her connivance even extended to leaving food where it could be spirited away with least risk of observation?

Such considerations, if they existed, never found their way into official records. But what we do know is that, having considerably helped to save the ship, they received no word of thanks, and equally, of course, no reward.

From 1815, however, we must go back half a century for our prize exhibit—the woman stowaway's account of her presence in the ship as told by herself to the men who knew of her entry and concealed her presence, and by them to the court-martial. If this broken illiterate narrative seems introduced with disproportionate

pomp and circumstance, in apology may be offered the fact of
its uniqueness—or its apparent uniqueness; at least an examination
of Naval courts-martial for the first three-quarters of the eighteenth century has turned up nothing similar, nor even remotely
comparable, in setting, events and characters.

On July 10, 1763, 'a Woman was found dead and sewed up in a
Hammacoe in the Bread Room on board of His Majesty's Ship
Defiance'. A week later, 'a Court Martial assembled on board His
Majestys Ship *Essex*, for inquiry into the cause [case], and for
trying' several men 'for being the Cause of her Death'.

And here at last the invisible woman becomes *officially* visible.
Moreover, of her kind, she represents the true stowaway, the
derelict unable to find a mouthful of bread ashore and obtaining
shelter at sea only by dint of tunnelling a mole's-run from ship
to ship, as the day of paying-off forced her from her hole; an un-
ending passage of darkness. The men who now come one by one
before the court-martial—a cross-section of every rank on the
ship—illuminate this chronic murk.

Henry Dearing, late Master-at-Arms of the *Defiance*, sworn:

I heard in the month of May last while the Ship was at Sea,
rumoured among the People between Decks that there was a
dead Woman in the Ship abaft down below. I know no more of
it.

The Master-at-Arms, as we have seen by the Regulations, was
responsible for the nightly patrol between decks. Dearing was the
officer, of all officers, who should have known of this illicit
passenger, yet 'he knew no more of it' till he had the news by
ship's grapevine—unless he were lying in his teeth.

Captain Mackenzie of the *Defiance*, sworn:

I ordered the Surgeon, the Master and the first lieutenant to go
down and Examine the Matter. The Corpse was examined by the
Surgeon.

John Dodgson, Surgeon, sworn:

Q. Did you survey the Body of this Woman?
A. I examined the Dead Woman carefully but did not observe any marks of violence.
Q. Had you heard of her being aboard and ill?
A. No, never.
Q. Did you inquire of your Mate [assistant] what Physick he had given her?
A. No. But I heard he gave her a Vomit, and bled her, and had given her some Opium.
Q. Could you have seen Externally, if the Opium had killed her?
A. No, unless she had been opened.

One of the men accused as being implicated in the death, now gives evidence. This is Christopher Gutteno, the Surgeon's Mate referred to above, who had attended the woman.

Gutteno, sworn:

She complained of being ill at her Stomach, and could keep nothing in her. I bled her and two days after gave her a Vomit, and the next day a Grain of Opium. I took all the care of her I could.

The second accused, Adam Rumbold, Purser's Steward, sworn:

We kept her private. She complained of a violent Head-Ach, we set up two Nights with her. I found her dead in the Morning about 5.

Then he offers the eye-witness testimony of such immense rarity: that the woman had been hidden aboard another ship, and smuggled into the *Defiance* by a seaman long since discharged from the ship. By putting the blame of concealment on this

unavailable person, he obviously hopes to escape the full responsibility for her presence.

The third accused, Thomas Hodges, seaman, sworn:

I know the woman had been hidden in another Ship before
coming aboard the *Defiance*. She had no watch [attendance] the
last night. I was present when she was sewed up, we were afraid
of being punished for concealing her.

By additional testimony of Rumbold and Hodges, this particular instance of stowing aboard took place not in an English port,
but on the West Indian Station.

And how had the men involved been discovered, out of the
Defiance's crew of hundreds? By a combination of primitive
detective work and monumental stupidity.

Captain Mackenzie:

I inquired how that Woman could have got in the Bread
Room, and who kept the Keys of that Room, on which it was
found that Rumbold habitually kept those Keys. He then
acknowledged that he had concealed her and that when she came on
board she was in good health. The reason for their not making any
report of the Death they said was, the fear of my punishing them.

VERDICT:
The Court agreed that the Woman died a natural Death and
that the Prisoners should be acquitted of being the Cause thereof.

Yet the verdict itself confuses, rather than terminates. Why is no
punishment mentioned for the seamen who concealed her? Why
no reprimand to the Master for his obvious laxity? Why no
censure, even, for the surgeon's mate who obviously connived at
the concealment by failing to report the woman's presence as
soon as her sickness made it known to him? He violated ordinary
discipline, if not his surgeon's oath. One more question comes to

mind, at random. Why not simply have weighted the body and dropped it over the side, instead of the unattractive conversion of the Bread Room into a burial vault?

Finally, from the stylized and orthodox court procedure, emerge two items by no means orthodox. The first is Thomas Hodges' quotation of some few hopeful words of the phantom as she composes herself to sleep after the surgeon-mate's final visit: 'She said if the Pill which the Doctor's Mate had given her would do her good, she should do well.'

The concluding item, more singular—possibly even momentous as implication, not event—is the court's complete lack of effort to identify the dead; to award it that last dignity of possession, a name of its own. The dead woman from first to last remained 'the Woman' wrapped in her winding-sheet of anonymity, as in her hammock-shroud.

The Visiting Prostitute

The sole cause and festering root of the system that regularly admitted prostitutes into a ship for longer or shorter visits was the absence, from Naval regulations, of any least provision for shore-leaves. Not only was such provision non-existent, it was—literally —unknown. In a day when part of almost every crew was secured by forcible impressment, every precaution was taken to ensure that the man aboard stayed aboard, once authority had succeeded in getting him there. The sole preoccupation of such men was to escape at all costs; that of commanders to defeat, at all costs, their natural urge to set foot once more on the blessed ground. Since the best chances for desertion came when the ship touched at various ports during her voyage, the only way of blocking such intentions was to anchor not at the dockside but a good mile or mile-and-a-half off shore. It was traditional that many seamen, wrenched from purely urban, rural or sedentary occupations, could not swim at all.

Briefly it might be noted that one or two commanders, as early as 1770, were so alive to the evil of penning men aboard ship for months that they instituted their own system of leaves, letting small groups ashore at a time. But these individual experiments, attempted at great risk to the commander himself, were less than a fleabite on the body of universal practice, having no connection whatever with routine Naval policy or practice.

The ship having anchored, it was understood tacitly that she became open house for the female professionals who had come swarming to the waterside from the first glad news of the ship's arrival. With the method for delivering this live freight into the ships, the first disfiguring scars of the system leap into prominence —the women's dependence on the boatmen who ferried them out, and the boatmen's unrestrained power of victimizing the women, according to set percentages of extortion. The seamen directly involved in the traffic—the purchasers of the commodity —will spell it all out for us and leave nothing unsaid. Yet, in their contemporary comment on an identical spectacle, may be seen a yawning gulf—that gulf which lies between the reaction and outlook of different generations. Extracts from these contemporary writings, again, will illuminate not only the custom, but developing public attitudes toward it. And illuminate, likewise, something even more remarkable: the extent to which permission or prohibition of the practice—vociferously recognized as a social monstrosity from 1800 onward—lay in the hands of the individual commander, as late as 1850.

This imposing upon the individual commander the heavy burden of deciding to treat with the plague according to his lights or his personal courage—of submitting, however violently it offended him, or of opposing what was universally practised and condoned—resulted once more from the stark failure of Regulations to acknowledge or adequately define the problem, from their earliest issue of 1731. Not till twenty-five years later does a scanty recognition of the visiting woman appear, and then in terms of one impotent prohibition, plus two feeble qualifications of its impotence.

Issue of 1756

That no Woman ever be permitted on board, but such as are really the Wives of the Men they come to; and the Ship not to be too much pestered even with them.

From this first (partial) statement of principle, might be attempted a graph of commanders' observance or interpretation of it, in terms of practice. And even if their innumerable experiences and comments were not available for quotation, their practice would be comment enough.

1788

Prince William Henry (William IV), then Admiral on the West Indian Station, issued the following to his commanders in port: *The command to see all strangers out of H.M.'s ships at gun-fire is by no means meant to restrain the officers and men from having either black or white women on board overnight, so long as the discipline is unhurt by the indulgence.*

The final qualifying phrase of the directive contains its weakness; who could tell in advance whether the 'indulgence' inflicted on the 'discipline' were an unimportant or a moral hurt? Other commanders' opinions on this point, up to William Henry's day, seem to minimize or ignore the question of eroded or destroyed disciplines, judging by the failure of *recorded* anti-measures. Even twelve years later, with the nineteenth century well up over the horizon and public moral awareness wider awake and touchier than before, still the commanders' view of the custom ranged between undisguised approval and vigorous opposition, with various shades of *laissez-faire* or amusement between; also officers were not wanting who perched uneasily on the fence. Among the few early resisters to the female take-over of the ship was that enterprising Captain of H.M.S. *Superb* who, in 1803, came up with a strikingly modern innovation:

In port, women will be permitted to come aboard upon the MEN BEING ACCOUNTABLE FOR THE CONDUCT OF THE WOMEN WITH THEM. *The Master-at-Arms will therefore keep a list, agreeable to the following form:*

Woman's Name	With Whom	When rec'd on board	CONDUCT

B

The dockside prostitute has created the printed form, an unlikely genesis. But again this order expressed only a qualified resistance, designed to curb the grosser forms of drunkenness and riot.

All the same may be traced—from these restrictions of the *Superb*'s Captain, which were in effect a compromise resistance—other resistances incomparably stiffer. In 1809 the great Collingwood issued a directive with as much compromise in it as the descent of an axe: 'Captain Carden has given permission for a number of women to come over in his ship', issued in steely accents from the Mediterranean Station. 'I have reproved him for this irregularity, and considering the mischief they make wherever they are, I have ordered them all to be conveyed to England again. I have heard there is a woman in the *Pickle;* send her out of the Fleet by the first transport.' By the allusion to mischief-making, he was almost certainly referring to a lower class of women than the wives, genuine or spurious, of the lesser or warrant rank of seamen.

Collingwood's iron accents were echoed two years later (1811) by Captain Cumby of the *Hyperion*: 'Every species of immorality is most peremptorily forbidden; the Master-at-Arms to see that no person sleeps out of his hammock.' Sharp voices and sharper orders pare away 'the indulgence' to vanishing point. That such voices are by no means a universal chorus, however, is proven by the antics (one may fairly call them that) of William Henry Dillon at various stages of his career.

This highly articulate man came aboard the *Camilla* as Acting Captain in 1809, and at once commented primly on her regular Captain Bowen's 'having with him a kept mistress, a companion that did not do much honour to his station'. Yet less than six months later his own ship, anchored at Spithead, was crammed with visiting girls as usual. Dillon now received instructions to proceed to Plymouth, and ordered the women ashore. At once the crew refused to unmoor the ship, a gesture of direct—or at best incipient—mutiny. But instead of threats to bring the nearest garrison aboard to restore order with the musket-butt, he had the ship's company assembled and made them a jolly man-to-man speech, pointing out that the fun was only postponed, as they could amuse themselves equally well at Plymouth. 'They then gave three vociferous cheers', he reminisces complacently, 'and unmoored the ship in double-quick time.' Dillon was a waverer, pulling offended faces at a captain's girl-friend, yet sustaining with perfect equanimity the invasion that reduced his own ship (as it did the proudest first-rate) to a shambles. Comparison of the two men's procedure—Collingwood's and Dillon's—reveals more than one point of irreconcilable conflict. What Dillon tolerated in 1809, Collingwood would not tolerate for a moment, also in 1809; that by mere accident of character-endowment Dillon could be threatened with mutiny, Collingwood with not a whisper of it; and that the shapeless mass of attitude and event converges sharply on proof that the matter still rested as much with the individual commander in 1809 as it had done in 1609 and 1709.

In 1822, however, a new and terrible witness steps forward, and his manner of entering upon the scene seems completely new. Houblon in 1677 protested, but in a private letter; Gibson in 1693 protested to the King personally and privately. But the anonymous man (or men) who wrote and published A STATEMENT OF CERTAIN IMMORAL PRACTICES IN H.M.'S NAVY, thrust the problem into broad daylight and made no bones about it.

This STATEMENT was a pamphlet of some sixty pages setting forth the experiences of the writer, and of four other Naval officers like himself, on H.M. ships in port unreservedly yielded up, by time-honoured custom, to the waterfront prostitute.

It is frequently the case that men take two prostitutes on board at a time, so that sometimes there are more women than men on board. The lower deck is already much crowded by the ship's own company; you may figure . . . the intolerable confusion and filth . . . when an addition of as many women as men is made to this crowd. Men and women are turned by hundreds into one large compartment, and in sight and hearing of each other shamelessly and unblushingly couple like dogs.

The pamphlet touches on the situation of the families of married seamen who wish to pay a visit while the ship is in port:

Wives and families, sometimes comprising daughters from 10 to 15 years of age, are forced either to witness these scenes, or to forego altogether the society of their husbands and parents. For all inhabit the same deck, huddled together whatever be their age or sex or character, eating, drinking and sleeping without any screen or separation between, and with every licentious propensity being unrestrainedly indulged.

Parents know nothing, he continues, of what they plunge their boys into when permitting them to enter the Naval Service:

The same abominations are going on in the midshipmen's births [sic]. A mid of 14 or 15 who had come on board only the day before, was thrust into bed with a prostitute by one of the lieutenants. It was the practice of the younger mids and boys to 'row guard' (as the expression was) between decks, seeking a connection with the superfluous women. Moreover they are ridiculed if they have not yet entered what God emphatically calls 'the paths of hell'.

The author now dares to mention, in this pamphlet accessible to the general public, the most cruel of the damaging effects:

The consequence is that two of the midshipmen contracted a foul disease, as well as many of the boys.

Allusion to the forbidden term conducts to the unexpected revelation that some commanders are attempting preventive measures; such attempts, though clearly sporadic, seem to indicate a state of modern medical practice already past its dawn:

Before the seaman is allowed to take his prostitute on the lower deck, IN MANY SHIPS it is insisted to get her examined by the assistant surgeon; if she is infected, she is sent out of the ship. But in one vessel, after every precaution was taken, one of these poor creatures died on board, of the venereal disease.

The response of Naval surgeons to this new duty illustrates a corresponding ambivalence of medical attitudes:

It must be mentioned, to the honour of the assistant surgeons in the Navy, that SOME *of them have resisted the order of their captains, and have chosen to brave the consequences rather than submit to actions so degrading.*

The pamphlet ends by entreating some official and permanent regulation to deal with the abuse misnamed 'the indulgence'.

So terrible a witness of the swarm and the pestilence, from sources at first-hand and above suspicion, would seem incontrovertible. Remarkable, therefore, to find it evoking powerful contradictions which—judging by their publication date of 1823 —must have been written at once, at top speed, and put on sale as fast as they could be printed and distributed. Their source was one of equal probity and experience—Anselm Griffiths, a retired Naval captain. In a gentlemanly and deliberate manner he skewers the writer of IMMORAL PRACTICES, then proceeds to carve him up. Although this person has chosen to be anonymous, he says with understated disdain, Captain Griffiths will not for that reason deny him the courtesy of believing that he tells the truth. 'But I have served in the Navy for over 30 years', he says in effect, 'and I have never observed comparable scenes, nor can I imagine the ship's officer who would permit them.' He then proceeds to his own experience of the practice, and this section is especially appealing for its fairness, good sense and down-to-earth humanity so classically typical of the officer-seaman.

Under the heading, *Women on Board*, he admits at once, 'This is an evil of considerable magnitude. The admission of 200 or 300 profligate women into a ship, is bad . . . but it is the practice of centuries and can plead long, very long, prescriptive custom'. Nor does he condemn the women wholesale. 'They do preserve as fair decency as you can expect.' Pathetic testimony of luckless creatures clinging to some last, inner shred of reserve in their struggle to escape the self-loathing of final abandonment. 'Any woman whose conduct is bad', he says, 'is turned instantly ashore', but hastily adds that immorality can never be justified. And now, in words that movingly reflect his resigned and indestructible compassion, 'The sailor's life is a very special one, and the remedy must not be applied violently or by rigid order. *You cannot make men moral by mere force of authority.* The zeal of the abolitionist should be tempered with judgment'.

And now that the topic has been thrust into public awareness as never before, it seems that outraged public opinion might impel, if not compel, some degree of official opposition. Yet, in actual practice, what was the result of the Statement and anti-Statement? One of unqualified failure, to judge by the after-effects; a momentary disturbance like a couple of stones flung into a fever-breeding pool, whose scummed surface closes over again at once. Even professional Naval opinion, for or against, is so little influenced that in 1829 and 1836—seven years and fourteen years after the pamphlets, respectively—we have two witnesses of this divergence at astonishing first-hand, and are even luckier to find them expressing the views of the very top, and the very bottom, of the Naval ladder.

The first and top-ranking instance (1829) we owe to Robert Wauchope, at that date a capable, popular and typical young officer, concerned exclusively with his prospects of promotion. He was then serving under an Admiral Plampin, 'a very immoral man living openly with a kept mistress who dined at his table'. Wauchope was apparently quite indifferent to this phenomenon when all at once, from some source within himself, he got a hard attack of religion. This was by no means the sour condemnatory variety, but consisted rather in an overwhelming sense of God's protectiveness and forgiveness. Under this influence he became sensitive to the presence of the illegal Mrs Plampin, and was rash enough to voice his objections to the Admiral. 'I told him that on reading the Bible, I found he was wrong.' Plampin received this revelation with the pleasure that might be expected, and began advertising Wauchope all over the Station as insolent, insubordinate or half-crazy, or all three.

Somewhere at this point the young man was invited by Sir Patrick Campbell to become his flag-captain, a brilliant offer and a decisive step toward the top. 'I accepted', Wauchope writes, 'on condition that prostitutes were not allowed to come aboard the ship.'

As no officer in his senses would bargain with promotion on

any terms—least of all for scruples over what was still a joke in many quarters—the gossip already spread about by Plampin was gloriously increased by this latest item, and in short order Wauchope found himself ordered to report to the Admiralty. With an excusable sinking of the heart he came up to London, and in his memoirs preserves the episode as we are lucky enough to have it. A piquant addition to the dialogue is the identity of the second participant: none other than Hardy, Nelson's Hardy, now First Sea Lord. The genial father of daughters who were forever sending him his favourite mince-pies, he was unrecognizable when disciplining a subordinate:

Hardy: I understand you object to women going on board?

Wauchope: I object to prostitutes going on board.

H.   You go contrary to the wishes of the Admiralty, and will therefore give up your commission.

W.   No. If the Admiralty choose to *take* my commission on this account, they may. I will not give it up.

H.   As one of the Lords of Admiralty, I consider it right that women should be admitted into ships; when I was sea, I always admitted them.

W.   Sir William Hoste never allowed it.

H.   Then he was very wrong, Sir.

W.   Captain Mande did the same.

H.   He did very wrong then, Sir. I do not wish to hear from you more upon this subject.

W.   [falling back on the stale old personal approach] Sir Thomas, would you allow *your* family to be exposed to such abominations?

H.   [gets out of it neatly and coldly] They never go aboard such ships, therefore they can't.

W.   Sir Thomas, it is written that *whoremongers shall not enter heaven.* Many officers hold the same opinions about admitting women aboard, as I do.

H.   I am sorry to hear it, Sir.

W.   When you view the subject deliberately, I hope you will agree with me.

H.   I hope I never shall, Sir. You have given up your
           commission.

But Wauchope appealed in other quarters; the commotion
died down, no more was heard of his losing his commission, and
he ended his career as Sir Robert Wauchope, Admiral of the
Blue. All this is told in his 'little book of memories' called
A Short Narrative of God's Merciful Dealings, and dedicated to
'my very dear grand nephew, Andy Wauchope'.

Now we plunge from highest to lowest, down the whole steep
slope of the Naval hierarchy; from an admiral's voice to the voice
of the lower deck heard almost never as an individual's, only as the
collective voice—the uproar—of mutiny. This solitary seaman's
voice belongs of course to Jack Nastyface, too well known to
the reader of Naval *mores* but perhaps less widely in a general
sense. Jack's pamphlet of 1836 completes as it were the gamut
of official opinion that has so far passed before us. We have seen
the fastidious officer repelled, the practical officer alarmed, the
cynical officer resigned or indifferent, the religious officer big with
solemn scriptural warnings. Jack exhibits, not surprisingly, the
pure lower-deck view, jaunty, relishing and callous—yet not
altogether, not entirely; beneath the ribaldry a faint breath of
regret escapes him, an instinctive sorrow before the spectacle of
defenceless poverty and its naked abuse, in sad combination.

'I can speak the truth with any man,' Jack declares, and goes
on to prove it.

'After having moored our ship, swarms of boats came around
us, a great many of them freighted with a cargo of ladies: a sight
truly gratifying, for our crew of 600 had seen but one woman in
18 months. So soon as these boats came alongside, the seamen
flocked down pretty quick and brought their choice up, so that
we had about 450 aboard.'

Here is one example where his natural kindness betrays him.

'Of all the human race, these poor young creatures are the
most pitiable; the ill-usage and degradation they are driven to
submit to, are indescribable; but from habit they become callous,
and so totally lost to all sense of shame, that they seem to retain

no quality which belongs to a woman, but the shape and name. On the arrival of any man-o-war in port these girls flock down to the shore, where boats are always ready.'

But others beside the girls have a money-stake in the game.

'As they approach the boat, the boatman surveys them from stem to stern; and carefully culls out the best-looking, and the most dashingly dressed, observing to one that she is *too old*; to another, she is *too ugly*; he will not be able to sell them, and he'll be damned if he has his trouble for nothing.'

Jack explains this selectiveness in terms of percentage. The boatman, beside his regular fare, gets three shillings of what the girl gets, and on a good day his takings may be five pounds. But if the cargo is too unattractive, 'officers have been known to lean over the rail and tell the boatman to push off with his lot of ugly devils; he will not allow his men to have them. The girls,' he adds, 'are not sparing of their epithets on such occasions'.

Some hours later, or perhaps next morning, word is given: all women ashore.

'A sailor here and there may seem to grieve for his Nancy, but most of them throw grief and a temporary affection over the taffrail. If a girl is unable to get up a few tears, the men offer her a couple of onions.' But the offer of a turnip at parting always implies dissatisfaction and disappointment with the girl's per- formance—a language of vegetables perfectly understood by anyone seeing it.

The ten last years of the scandal evidence its unchanging double- headed nature, its tenacious inconsistencies and incongruities; as officers fight more and more to abolish the privilege of centuries, the seamen fight all the more to retain it. Between 1840 and 1850, constant outbreaks of mutiny in the British Navy arose from this one cause, efforts of prohibition. One captain, refusing to allow women into his ship at Portsmouth, received from his admiral a rebuke so blistering that apparently it has not been allowed to survive, even in modified form. In a century already familiar with trains, telegrams, mechanized industry, electric light and anaesthesia, ships in port are still overrun with 'sailors' wives', an ancient slang term. At times the monster seems in its death-throes,

B*

at other times it demonstrates there is plenty of life left in its coils.

All the same, though seemingly undiminished in force of numbers, the waterfront bawd is mysteriously withdrawing into the shadow of things past, worked on by forces of attrition which no animate nor inanimate thing can, in the end, resist. And yet she maintains, in her very withdrawal, the enigma of her contradictions. Up to the very end her destitution, her pitiable finery, her ignorance, have seemed to triumph brazenly all over the English Naval tapestry; to have emerged, in her running battle with epaulets and gold lace, as invincible. No enactment of Admiralty has obliterated her, for such enactments have existed for twenty years; against official and other protests, she seems to have conquered.

And yet an unsuspected opponent has been working against her. The wiping out of the evil has seemed to wait on the fusion of resistances, of increased public awareness, and ultimately on workings of Admiralty. But perhaps reform has waited, even more, on that mysterious process by which the most acrid and noisiest contention drops into the dark hole which is Time, overnight; falls to silence and oblivion for no clearer reason than that its span of life has run out, and its natural end has come.

Wives Aboard

The restless chapter of the legal or nearly-legal spouse at sea, through its freedom from the disfiguring tragedy of the stowaway's or visiting whore's life, is the only one in which may be found a measure of light relief. Allusions to officers' wives living aboard permanently or semi-permanently exist from 1600; by the eighteenth and nineteenth centuries it will be seen how frequently and casually admirals, captains and first lieutenants took their wives aboard without the formality of asking permission. Over the years the delicate question of genuine or spurious matrimony crops up fitfully, but never so as to constitute a serious or lasting impediment. From earliest times Naval authorities existed who considered the custom a nuisance, but their efforts at interference chop and change so distractedly that they elude any meaning in sequence; one has a powerful impression that, in the end, such reformers were glad to let the whole thing drop. Little wonder, for the manifestations of these ladies were erratic beyond anticipation and childish beyond punishment; not the deep sinister fouling of the woman outcast, but the delicate random scratches of a hopping bird.

About 1625, for example, curious reports of powder-shortages were constantly noted in a certain small ship. She had not been on war service, on the contrary she had been anchored a long time in the Medway, yet her stores of powder continued to show mysterious deficiencies. Nemesis was a long time coming, but caught up at last. The ship's gunner, relentlessly questioned, confessed that he had fallen into the practice of firing salutes whenever an officer or his wife went ashore. Whether this had begun as a joke, or in consequence of some individual's idea of his own worth, the custom had seeped down to the warrant officers, then to the warrant officers' wives. Since no one who had ever received this intoxicating dignity would ever agree to give it up, the gunner's amiable weakness let it continue; every time a purser's wife went ashore to knock back a pint with a crony, a one-gun salute informed a waiting world of the fact. At the end of the investigation a deathly silence from the ship replaced what the seaman Duke of Clarence called 'these continual poppings'.

In January, 1627, the St Lawrence had been in port for some interval not stated. Her storekeeper (variously named, by the unjelled spelling of the period, as Croshoe, Crashaw or Crawshaw) was living aboard with his wife. Obviously she would know the storerooms well, and during one of her husband's absences was using her knowledge to steal supplies out of the ship —whether with or without his connivance is not stated. The thefts at any rate were conspicuous enough to result in discovery by one Captain Thom. Watt, on a tour of inspection for the Lord High Admiral. Reporting to this eminent being, 'my most honoured Lord the Duke of Buckingham', Watt reports exhaustively on important matters like wages and sickness, then drops to pettier concerns: 'I have sent to Mr Nicholas [the Duke's secretary] an inventory of such provisions as were imbeaseled out of the St Lawrence by Croshoe his wife in his absence. The relation whereof,' he concludes with weary disgust, 'being too teadious for Y° Grace, Mr Nicholas may inform you of it.' If the husband had encouraged the thieving wife, recriminations might be mutual; if not, Croshoe his wife probably got the thrashing she deserved.

The next example, amusing on the surface, hides a contravention of authority definable as treason, and certainly eligible for court-martial. In June, 1628, a fleet of three ships at Portsmouth was ordered to the siege of Rochelle. Days followed, and still the ships did not sail. Excuse after excuse was given; necessity of repairs, water supplies not arriving, and so forth. At last Secretary Coke, by some means unknown, unearthed the real reason, and wrote grimly to Buckingham, 'They mean not to haste away, who have sent for their wives on board'. Remarkable instance of concealed but virtual refusal, by Naval ships, of war orders; holding up departure on various pretexts, till the ladies arrived.

Evidences of women are strangely frequent in what was called Cromwell's Navy—the Navy created out of Charles I's unresting efforts, and reduced by Cromwell to the more indecent stages of bankruptcy before his death. These female elements appear in all ranks from highest to lowest, nor does their capricious character make them less pleasing. In May, 1648, for example, seven ships were lying in the Downs. Their Admiral was anti-royalist, their seamen were Royalist, and feeling between the Admiral and crews was not cordial. Imprudently the Admiral went ashore on business; on attempting to come back, 'he found that his ships would not receive him'. Moreover the non-reception committee had prepared another surprise, having loaded 'his wife and children into a small vessel', where he was forced to join them, and the whole party was rowed ashore and unceremoniously dumped. Curious testimony—by eviction—of a whole family ensconced in a warship, though it lay at anchor. Another wife aboard left her fleeting mark upon an episode ten years later, when Captain Jeremy County commanded a Commonwealth ship in a fight with the *Lepauldus*; apparently the engagement was indecisive, and a Naval colleague, one Captain Heaton, began spreading malicious talk about the reasons for this semi-failure. Captain County, getting wind of these aspersions, wrote to the Admiralty in such a rage that he hardly took time for the customary salutations: 'Captain Heaton stated . . . *that my wife's being on board was the cause I did not further engage.*' Lethal accusation—that a ship's commander avoided combat for the sake of his wife's safety. 'Concerning my wife', he continues furiously, 'I had not a thought of her during the time, I never saw her or spoke to her or of her, until we hauled in our guns', and his voice has the ring of truth. But unwittingly he portrays for us the commander's wife during battles at sea; banished to her lonely cabin in ignorance of what was happening till the ship won, or was set ablaze by cannon-fire, or captured, or sunk.

Up to the eighteenth century references to our specific field are sparse and tentative, a sort of exhausted sop thrown to convention. By 1703, however, they take on a new lease of life along with their allusion to a new and restless debate; again not among top authorities, only in the bosoms of individual commanders with regard to a special class of ship. By a regulation of January 1, 1703, the Sick and Wounded Board permitted 'every Hospital Ship to have Six Nurses and Four Laundresses, none under the age of Fifty Years'. Having guaranteed the celibate life by means of this barrier, they go on to the wistful query, 'And whether they should not all be Seamen's Wives, or Widows, and have Ordinary Seamen's pay?'

Treading hard on the heels of this proposal—six days later in fact—Sir George Byng, inspecting hospital ships, comes up with another brilliant suggestion: 'Instead of Women, Men to be Allways employed.' With similar promptitude (February, 1703) a War Council headed by Admiral Penn puts a foot down hard: no shipboard employment for any woman, wife or no wife. This sweeping prohibition made women scarce for a while, obviously, for a Naval commander quickly added a sad and warning note: that many sick and wounded men have died who would not have died if women had remained in the ships to take care of them, and that men in general were not suited for nursing. From the patients themselves came, with even more emphasis, indications that the fevered brow was not soothed by the touch of a horny palm, and a couple of years later (1705) we find the inevitable corollary: women are back in the ships as 'nurses and Laundresses' and carried regularly on the ship's books as paid crew.

To the tussle of the Cromwellian Navy a special piquancy is added, considering the tenacious Puritan halo. Surely from these stern and incorruptible uplifters a purifying influence must spread through all ranks and reform even the most unregenerate lower deck, the hardest-bitten seaman? The actual story adds its bit of tarnish to the halo. One of its outstanding features seems to be that Protectorate measures in regard to women aboard deal most often with an ostensibly respectable woman, the warrant officer's wife. The inference seems to be that this particular class had become numerous enough to be conspicuous, while to some authorities their usefulness was less apparent than their talent for making trouble. One groping attempt to restrict their numbers was a stipulation: that if these wives supplied their own food for the voyage, they might go along as nurses or laundresses. But the coincidental and rising rate of venereal disease made it clear that such vestals were by no means dedicated solely to the sickbed and the washtub, and further Interregnum attempts at restriction display a progressive anaemia of invention.

As on the trampled and re-trampled battlefield of the undisguised prostitute, the newer ground of nurses and laundresses saw sharper and severer collisions as the nineteenth century approached. A dire trump was sounded when Captain Cochrane, a strict Methodist, assumed command of his ship in 1793. The first act of this killjoy was 'to ascertain whether all women on board were married, and their certificates were demanded. A few of the seamen *were* married', the narrator concedes. 'The others had nominal wives—an indulgence generally winked at in the Navy'. But winking was not Cochrane's way, and his demand for marriage lines 'created a very unpleasant feeling among the tars'. This massive understatement and all the rest of it we owe to our old friend Captain William Henry Dillon, last seen talking his crew out of mutiny at Spithead.

Now, with the nineteenth century proper—as if in the year 1800 lay buried an accelerated beat of a tocsin—allusions come with a rush; thick, fast and variegated, also in a language more familiar and direct, speaking more plainly to our emotions. The higher officer's wife figures conspicuously in these references, which include her husband's explanation, at first hand, for her presence aboard. Of these the chief and most appealing, in the first rank of command, was loneliness. Since a principal element in controlling those under him was his power to inspire awe, by instruction and custom the ship's captain lived in a sort of royal isolation, alone at his meals and alone in his leisure; bound to a rigorous formality of address to his officers, friendship or ward-room companionship equally banned to him. The complete success of this practice is seen in the classic image of the sea-captain, a figure whom his subordinates trembled to approach. This does not imply that the captain enjoyed his freezing solitude, whose only practical alleviation was the companionship of his wife.

Other commanders took their wives to sea for reasons much more diverting. Chief among these is the irrepressible Dillon—now Captain Sir William Henry Dillon—who bobs up to explain with complete frankness and nonchalance the presence of his wife in the *Leopard* troopship. He had married a widow not long before, and woken up too late to her irresponsible and ruinous extravagance. By the stratagem of penning her in the ship he could at least make sure she was not running up bills—and make sure equally of not being arrested for her debts the moment he set foot in England. Accordingly he suggested a voyage to Lady Dillon; she liked the idea momentarily and came aboard complete with luggage, lady's maid and a daughter by a previous marriage. The *Leopard* was not sailing on combat duty but only carrying troops; nevertheless she was an H.M. ship on war service, and the captain's wife and step-daughter were enjoying a lengthy cruise in her at the State's expense. At this very time Dillon's second lieutenant was resisting transfer to another ship, and Dillon explains why with the same engaging tranquillity: 'He had his wife permanently with him, and wished not to be in any cruising [active duty] ship.'

The principal target of new resistances to the sea-going house-hold was the lower or warrant-officer's wife (boatswain's, purser's, etc.) of whom an enormous floating population existed. Presumably in such cases the captains had given permission, but to judge by what came to the surface in the final instance, and by the Admiralty's own admission, they seldom withheld it. The explanation here was simpler and even more basic than the stresses acting on commanders. Petty officers were poorly and in-frequently paid, unable to maintain their wives on land or get money to them when they needed it; if they had no young family, the most practical step was for the wife to make her home in the ship in port or afloat. The economic lash drove the legal and illegal spouse aboard with equal force, but in this mixed bag—recalling St Vincent's fury against them on the lethal count of wasting precious water-supplies, and in a war area at that—it may be recalled likewise that even he made no attempt to sort out the sheep from the goats, knowing too well the alternatives for both classes: the near-starvation level or death from hunger in the streets.

The pyramiding evidences and resistances so far offered in the case of the poorer wife or so-called wife reach an apex—a culmination of testimonies—in a corner more dimly lit by the blaze of Nelson's two greatest sea-epics. After the Battle of the Nile (1798) two women, Ann Hopping and Mary Anne Riley, applied for the medals being awarded for this action; Jane Townsend in the *Defiance* at Trafalgar (1805) also applied, 'presenting strong and highly satisfactory certificates of her useful services during the combat'. These applications, with others from women, were all turned down by the Admiralty. On what grounds? '*That many women in the Fleet were equally useful.*' But the mean and grudging official refusal also reveals that—for all the absolute prohibition of women in warships—their tenure was as flourishing and undisturbed as ever. The nature of their 'useful services during combat' may be seen in a painting by Thomas Stothard, a ship's deck at full battle-heat; the two women present, not featured nor dramatized in any way, blend into sweating straining groups, doing men's work among men. One of these

ACCOMMODATION.
OR
Lodgings to Let at Portsmouth!!

John Nicol, Mariner in the Hulks

makes up the team of five required to serve a cannon, all five faces equally lurid in the glare of its discharge. The other, bent double almost invisibly in the left-hand corner, tries to drag a fallen officer aside; from no sentiment overt nor implied, only because—in the rush and trample of combat—there is no time for tripping over corpses. Perhaps the woman working demoniacally in the cannon's very mouth, and the one striving with the big man's dead weight, are examples of those rejected for medals.

From 1805 the poorer wife's permanant or semi-permanent tenure aboard ship might be conjectured as equal to the prostitutes'—roughly another forty to forty-five years. Sheltering behind a respectability actual or ostensible, she created no such problems as her more unlucky and turbulent sisters, the pestilent waterfront scenes of girls crowding into boats against an accompaniment of screams and obscenities from those rejected by the boatmen; nor had her presence ever inspired the riots and near-mutinies consequent on commanders resisting invasion by waterfront whores, disturbances forever increasing as resistances increased. After Nile and Trafalgar the 'usefulness' of these strong weatherbeaten women during major battles was admitted even by the Admiralty, without—to its shame—a shred of recompense for them, or even acknowledgment. No cause of conspicuous disorders, admittedly valuable at times, they called for no specially harsh directives to keep them in control.

A frequent job for women, during combat, seems to have been rushing ammunition to the guns. But by testimony of the artist who painted the canvas at the Maritime—and surely by its starkness he was depicting something he had seen—other women qualified as more direct instruments of war. The gaunt creature seen in the inferno of discharging cannon is stripped of all outward femininity, a mere unit of the five-man team labouring in smoke, sweat and powder-reek; labouring also cheek by jowl with death near the iron monster's deafening roar and recoil and its metal heating up, more and more dangerously, toward the point of possible explosion.

The Woman in the Hulks

The ships used for transportation of convicts, and called hulks, were actually Naval ships retired from regular service. In this connection the experiences of women in them might be described briefly but at close quarters, since information of this sort is—surprisingly—available to us.

A female prisoner destined for Botany Bay or Port Jackson via the hulks would, if she had sense or luck, form an immediate association with one of the seamen aboard. Apparently it was policy never to mix transported criminals of both sexes, so that women would be in a ship for women only; but in the crew of hundreds there would be the inevitable vicious element. Putting herself under the protection of one particular seaman shielded her more or less from the nocturnal prowler alone or in gangs, with the possible corollary of mass rape and a dead girl (or apparently dead) being dropped overboard in the night watches. Added to this consideration of safety was another, the prospect of sharing her protector's rations which—vile as they were—looked Epicurean beside the swill given the convicts, and which made the crammed lower decks a hell of disgusting sicknesses, prostrations and death.

To the same fluke that impelled an illiterate man like Nastyface to put his life on paper, and to the fluke of such writings surviving instead of being lost as so much is lost, we owe *Adventures of a Mariner*. Just as Nastyface is a witness at first hand for the visiting whore, John Nicol, author of *Adventures*, is a witness for the transported female convict. He wrote with natural ease and power of expression, and presumably his publisher cleaned up his spelling and grammar before the book went to press. One phase of his experience was serving as seaman in the convict ship *Lady Julian* in 1789, only eleven years before the nineteenth century.

The prisoners in Nicol's ship were lucky (if the word is not too far-fetched) in being spared the savage and indecent crowding in men's hulks. Only 245 women and girls were aboard, and to supply this number, he tells us, 'all the gaols in England had been emptied out' and dumped into the *Lady Julian*. A few such prisoners had been receivers, shop-lifters, forgers of powers of attorney and impersonators (for the purpose of fraudulently claiming dead seamen's pay). These were the aristocrats. 'The greater number were harmless unfortunate creatures, the victims of seduction', practically all of them sentenced for petty theft or street-walking or both.

'They all came aboard in irons', Nicol recalls. He had the job of knocking off their shackles, with extra pay for doing so. Once aboard, it was compulsory that they should change into convict dress. The captain of any hulk was empowered to throw overboard all attire remaining from days of freedom, but the captain of *Lady Julian* was either humane or indifferent and let them keep their dresses and small finery. Among the crowd were the noisy and troublesome few, but none dangerous; whether this was the rule or the exception, Nicol does not specify. One irrepressible spirit got up on the quarter-deck, flounced and strutted in mockery and defiance, and was carried down kicking and clawing with undiminished enthusiasm. She got a dozen of the cat; Nicol is so casual about the episode that we may guess the punishment as not horrible nor permanently destructive—not as in men's floggings where it was mandatory that a thick curl of skin and flesh should follow each blow of the lash, or the flogger would get the same himself.

A number of women came aboard pregnant, or became pregnant during the voyage, or claimed to be pregnant whenever the ship touched in for stores or water, such pretences being for good and profitable reasons. News of a hulk carrying female passengers seemed to bring the more tender-hearted and wealthier ladies of the place flocking to the ship for purposes of alleviation; this was apparently a recognized, even a fashionable, form of charity. The chief efforts of these benefactresses were directed at the woman presently or prospectively in childbed, and by claiming this condition a girl came in for a share of bedlinen, medicines, delicacies and alms. Other rackets, naturally, flourished aboard ship. In the *Lady Julian*, Nicol tells us, was a group of Jewesses who had crucifixes and rosaries, and who did remarkably well out of commiserating Catholics ashore.

Prisoners' victualling was different from that of crews. For breakfast was given an evil-smelling porridge of oatmeal or barley gone so bad, in hot weather, that eventually it had to be dumped, even the pigs aboard refusing it. Soup from spoiled salt beef, peas, cheese and small beer completed the menu. Bread or biscuit were made of bran and damaged rye flour. This second mention of spoiled barley and spoiled barley-product recalls the ergot poisoning from mildewed barley called, in the Middle Ages, St Anthony's Fire, and is consistent with its effects in the hulks— skin conditions that drove the prisoners frantic, and exhausting diarrhoea. The latrines were near the sleeping quarters and were unsupplied with water. Convicts would wrench off their clothes and stand at the portholes, gasping for a breath of air. The high death-rate was unimportant, since delivering the cargo in good condition was not the captain's concern; his responsibility ended with landing it at its destination, or proving which of its number had died en route.

Nicol is a first-hand example of the temporary relationships among crews and passengers, since he had 'taken under my protection, during the tedious voyage' one such girl, who more-over had borne him a son in course of the year-long journey. He says he wanted to marry her, and there is no reason to dis-believe him. In later years he tried to find some trace of her and the child, but never heard of them again. Such pathetic associa-tions were inevitably doomed to one ending; the girl was bound by her sentence, the man bound to his ship's return voyage. Failure in either case reduced the girl's status to escaped convict, the man's to Naval deserter, both implacably hunted and bound to undergo—if caught—a worsening of their condition beyond all imagination.

But even more than in his desire to make an honest woman of his luckless Emily, John Nicol's kind and sensitive heart shines out in his exchanges with another girl aboard the convict ship. Her words must have sunk deep to enable him to set down at such length an utterance so completely unlike his own style, in its fiery heat and intensity. Answering his query whether she minded her banishment from England:

'Banished!' she spat at him. *'Have we not been always banished, while yet in our native land?* We dared not go to our relations whom we had disgraced, they would shut their doors in our faces. We were hated and shunned. When we rose in the morning we knew not where we would lay our heads in the evening. We knew not if we would break our fast in the course of the day. We were at the mercy of every drunken ruffian. Banished!' she annihilated him. 'Our banishment is a *blessing!*' and the eloquence of her answer sheds a faint gleam on an unrelated and buried tale—the presence as witnesses, at Naval courts-martial, of prostitutes. 'They gave their evidence well, even very well', says an officer of 1780. He was obviously surprised that it should be so. But this mental power and promptness in women considered the gutter-leavings of society affords a view of intelligences never given a chance, but revealing themselves for one moment as potentially useful, even remarkable; a blasted heath rolling endlessly back-ward through centuries, of loss and waste.

And the last of the woman at sea, the high officer's, petty officer's and seaman's wife, what was it? The last of the visiting whore and her rarely-glimpsed sister stowed in lower-deck darkness, her life and her death secret: what were their final endings? By what precise compulsions, in the nineteenth century, did the Queen's Navy purge itself of the immemorial presence in its various shapes and forms?

As for wives of whatever degree, high or low, the tightening Navy regulations of 1847, plus changing social attitudes, brought matters to a point where no officer, even admirals and captains, would risk a showdown with the Admiralty on this count. Domesticity afloat vanished entirely by about 1860, its disappear-ance—like its tenure—unsensational, even ladylike.

Of that rare and hidden variety—the woman below, never venturing to show herself in the light of day—her obliteration is as silent, as unrecorded, as herself. The same official reticence that denied her even to the extent of not forbidding her presence, pre-vailed to the last. Faceless and nameless in her beginning, she remains the same in her ending—yet this shadowed and indeterminate ending illustrates, perhaps, the paradox of causes operating powerfully, which are not *directly* related to their effects.

One such partial and conjectural cause may be in certain amendments of Regulations, dated 1824, on the subject of cleanliness. This was nothing new; as early as 1756-57 we find instructions that 'the Men do constantly keep themselves as clean as possible: that the Ship be always kept thoroughly clean'. The theory was good, the practice nil. Forty years later St Vincent commented that 'the men's woolens, once put on, are never washed or changed till they rot off', while the bunks alive with typhus lice that he and Dr Baird ripped out of ships as late as 1798, were a commonplace shipboard condition.

In 1824, however, the old flabby rules on cleanliness were suddenly strung up tight, with disheartening notes of strictness and particularity. 'The men must wash themselves twice a week, and change their linen twice every week.' A dirty man is now punished, and in 1833 the punishments are stressed and repeated.

So it may be that, with this insistence on cleanliness, and the severe and frequent inspections it entailed, it became more and more impossible to hide a woman aboard and keep her hidden. New techniques of discipline, of shipbuilding and lighting were sweeping away—with other dim romantic squalors—the savage, beautiful, filthy, heart-breaking world of the great wooden sailing-ship. Cleaned out were the fetid holes where a seaman's Nancy lay on a bed of rags, sharer of maggoty rations, seasickness and terror of discovery. Therefore, it seems possible that the vanishing of this forlorn spectre had a bizarre alliance with new hygienic practice, revolutionized Naval architecture and electric light.

For the most conspicuous and troublesome class of ship's prostitute—the temporary visitor—the lines of demarcation between indulgence and prohibition are most waveringly drawn of all. Individual oppositions to the practice, passing before us from 1800 on, continued their dubious and ineffectual progress as far into the new century as its sixth decade; with such creeping gait does humanity advance.

But now, in 1861[1] the Admiralty instituted, as routine practice, the giving of regular shore-leaves. With one stroke of the pen were abolished the scabrous waterfront scenes, the hundreds of women whose frantic jostling and fighting for places in the boats was merely an exercise in survival; the ruthless selections of the boatmen against a chorus of screams and imprecations from the rejected. Abolished by the same measure, likewise, was the volcanic mutiny-and-riot potential of men penned in the ship for perhaps a year, with no single moment of freedom on land. That the seaman was better fed, better lodged, clean and promptly paid and emancipated from flogging and other mutilations, must assuredly and immeasurably have improved the Service. Beyond this however, and above all, was the effect of the 1861 innovation on the ancient, perennial and enormous problem of desertions. The Naval seaman, now guaranteed—at least by rotation—some hours of shore liberty wherever the ship touched in, was delivered from the pent-up crazes of the cage that drove him to break free at all costs.

To the fact of the double conquest of the double plague, effected by the pen's single stroke, the records of Admiralty testify almost at once. The 'run man', the deserter, no longer fills its pages with descriptions and grim unsleeping pursuit, with his fugitive's aura of sweat and fear. The ship's-side harlot and the run man, two accusing ghosts, seem to vanish side by side into some charnel murk thick with the victims of old inhumanities, forever defenceless, forever unavenged.

In this submerged chronicle of the sea-going woman must remain, of necessity, areas forever sunk from sight or conjectural, displacements of time and tide suggested but not proven. Of her disappearance, we know that it comes under the blanketing term of 'reform'. What Boscawen and others tried to do for their men and could not do because they were a hundred years ahead of their generation, was done by improvements not directly aimed at the reform they brought about.

[1] For all information on shore leaves the writer is indebted to Lieutenant-Commander P. K. Kemp, Admiralty Archivist (retd), who generously allowed her to consult the MSS. of a book of his, then in preparation.

But however that may be, somewhere in the British Navy—on some day not recorded, from some ship not named—the last crinoline of the captain's lady, the last coarse skirt of the warrant-officer's wife, the last verminous curl and bedraggled frill of the visiting or stowaway whore, went down a ship's gangway for the last time. And not till that moment, perhaps, has the eighteenth century really come to an end.

II

DISTRESS'D WIVES

WIVES of seafaring men, left destitute through no fault of their husbands, throng the Papers in greater numerical proportion, perhaps, than any other class of person. Some were the wives of officers, women bred up to a fair standard of living and education; some were wives of common seamen, partly or wholly illiterate and born to the hardest, barest existence. But the differences of birth and breeding that ordinarily raise one woman above another are soon ground to nothing, or less than nothing, under the heel of economic pressure. Different in background and social position, identical in poverty, their similar anxieties extorted from their voices a similar note of human misery. This composite begging voice is preserved to us in the only recourse of such women—the petition—and no day passed on which King, Council or Admiralty were not faced with two or three documents of this sort; their numbers, if tallied straight through the Papers, would be in thousands and perhaps tens of thousands.

The petition, most frequently used between 1600-1700 as a recognized instrument of request, was governed by conventions that must have been well-defined in its day but are less distinct to ours. On reading a number of them certain differences seem to emerge, but cannot be absolutely counted on. For instance, fifty or sixty petitions may appear to demonstrate that only a wife or widow of a ranking officer was entitled to petition the King direct. Later exceptions, however, prove this not to be true, but the exceptions—from wives of common seamen—are likely to take the form of mass petitions. Again, within a certain period we find countless appeals to the then Lord High Admiral, the Duke of Buckingham, as an intermediary to the King rather than to the King direct, but both varieties demonstrate an interesting difference of approach. Where men often petitioned Council, the women aimed straight at the more personal targets of the King, his favorites or his highest officers; and yet, woman sometimes petitioned impersonal authority such as the Council or the Lords of Admiralty.

The very abundance of this material, an embarrassment of riches, imposes its own necessity of selecting those which seem most remarkable; no easy task, because all are remarkable. The outcry of stark need is always arresting, but with all its sameness it may ring with individualities of timbre, as when an extremity of despair forces from a woman an extremity of eloquence, which at ordinary times would not be possible to her. Nor does this painful eloquence necessarily proceed from the more educated woman; sometimes it is the obviously illiterate one who wrests, out of her meagre resources of speech, a very consummation of entreaty. Whether wives or widows, all had been left in frightful poverty through the absence of the provider forced away on long voyages or killed in the service; perhaps the very largest class were those whose husbands, captured by Barbary or Dunkirk pirates, had been sold as slaves in Algiers (called Barbary or Sallee). All such women were eligible for relief—in theory. For the woman with small children was reserved, certainly, the deepest hell.

The first requirement of the petition was that it had to be short, and the lower the petitioner's social standing, the shorter. In appearance these documents are mere strips of parchment about three inches wide by five or six long, written the long way of the paper. All are done in professional scrivener's copperplate, and all represent an expense in preparation and registration that most petitioners could ill afford. The mandatory salutation and termination, always the same, are quoted only once. Examples are greatly abridged and not in chronological order; an introductory composite of the style is given before going on to petitions of a more special or unusual nature. An inexact attempt has been made to trace a straight line in rising degrees of rank.

TO THE KINGES MOST EXCELENT MAIESTIE

The humble petition of [...*name*...], the Distress'd Wife of [...*name*...]

Humbly sheweth, that pet^r Husband, late [...*rank*...] aboard Y° Maties Shipp [...*name*...], kill'd on [...*date*...] at [...*place of battle*...], leaving her a distress'd Widowe with [...X...] small Children destitute of Livelyhood and readie to perrish for want

That Y° Maiestie would be pleased out of th' aboundance of pitie, to order some reliefe for the said [   ] and hir small children

And Y° Pet^r will ever pray as in dutie bound, for Y° Mat^{ie} long lyfe, health and happye raygne

Beside exhibiting the common ground of fear, hunger and want, the wives of Barbary captives often mention their exertions on behalf of their husbands.

Humbly shewinge that the pet^r husband was taken by pyrates to Sallee, where hee now lyeth in woefull miserrie and is like to continue in p'petual bondage

May it please Y° Lo^{pps} [Lordships] to pitie her distressed estate in the absence of her husband

And that Y° Lo^{pps} good favoure to him be extended, and that you would give present [immediate] order for his releasement

In other words, she begs that they will pay ransom so that her husband can be freed. These redemptions, in the language of the day, were called 'emptions'.

The following petition throws light upon the cost of such emptions. It also reveals that if the price were not forthcoming from public or ecclesiastical funds, the wife took it on herself to scrape up the money where and how she could.

The humble petition of Margaret Praulfe. Her husband hath long been prisoner with the Turkes, for whose release she hath long been a miserable suitor. Upon her petition to the Lords [of Admiralty?] they refeard [referred] her to the L° B^p [Lord

Bishop] of Canterbury, who will but alow £50 for his redemption, which cannot bee had under £200. Shee hath been well descended and lived plentifullie, but now is miserable and humbly petitioneth for letters to collect for his redemption in diverse Countries [counties].

By 'letters' she means licence. Raising money by public solicitation of any kind, down to begging in the streets, was very strictly licensed. A mass effort for ransom is seen in a petition of October 15, 1636, where numbers of women pray for 'a License for a Collection throughout England and Wales, for the redeeming of poore English men, Captives under Muley Abda Wally, King of Moroccoe'. In what manner did these wives collect? By begging from door to door or in the street, holding out a bowl to passers by, who had already seen and heard more than enough of such entreaties?

The heartbreaking length of time that a suit could drag on is told by

Rebecca Burton, widdow. [Her petition has been seen by Council, who pass it on with a note in the margin: they wish the King would do something for her to end her suit, which she has been bringing for ten years.]

The joint petition of two or three women is very usual; evidently Constance Griffin, Mary Dixon and Ann Cookery put their scanty resources together, instead of each one bearing the whole cost of the application. But the full force of the mass petition—in terms not only of the misery it represents, but of the numbers of kidnapped Englishmen—has hardly been felt, until the following:

TO THE DUKE OF BUCKINGHAM HIS GRACE

The humble peticon of the Distress'd wives of almost 2000 poore Mariners now remayninge most miserable captives confinned in Sally in Barbary. Where not only themselves suffering unspeakable tortures, but Y° Pet^{rs} with a multitude of poore Infants are ready to perish here at home, from want of means;

ffrom whence they are altogether void [penniless] for the redemption of their poore Captives.

They now explain why they have addressed themselves to the Duke.

Y° poore Pet^{rs} have exhibited [offered] many peticons already to his royall Matie, but could never get answer.

Now comes the awful part:

[The petitioners] have many letters from their husbands, wherein they write that the least letter or signifycacon from his Matie would procure their enlargement [release].

Did James, not a bad sort of man, actually never bestir himself in an urgency so frightful? But apparently not, and now these wives' last hope is to persuade Buckingham to persuade the King.

Their most humble sute is, That Y° Grace in your wonted goodnes and pitty toward poore Women, would be gratiously pleased for God's Cause to move his Matie, in his pious and princely compassion, for the redeeming and relieving of their said Husbands.
And as bound, shall ever pray etc.

More special and individual is a variation of the mass petition brought in March, 1631.

The most humble petition of Alice Gibson the distress'd wife of James Gibson Marriner in the good Shipp called the *Transport of London* under the Comaund of Captain West.

Alice goes on to retail her distracting bad luck. The *Transport* had captured a French ship called the *Marie of Clona* [?]. Seamen in the *Transport*, by usual custom, would get their share of the captured ship's value, which was called prize-money. But the money being long in coming—apparently—an unusual thing happened: the ship's company of the *Transport* visited Alice, begged her to take legal steps to get their money for them, and in return promised 'that Y° Pet^r should receive 12d out of every single share'. The action of the seamen is understandable: they probably had not a penny with which to fight their battle, and perhaps were illiterate into the bargain.

Alice must have had some small means, for she petitioned on their behalf—this is virtually unknown, a woman representing an entire ship's company—and actually after eleven months, obtained their money by an Admiralty Court order. The 'marriners' played fair: 'they did leave such summes of money as was agreed in Court, in Captain Westes hands for ye pet^r'.

But having won the case for others, Alice's troubles were just beginning: 'when y° pet^r did demaund of the said West the said money due to her, he in verye evill words (not fitt to be uttered) would not pay such money due to her for her eleven moneths paines and charges'. For which reason, Alice is now in no flourishing way:

Y^r Pet^r said husband is gone to the East Indies and hath been absent almost two years, by which meanes she is almost readie to perish for want of supportacon, and unable to [recover] her right by lawe of the said West. Wherefore in all prostrate humilitie shee most humbly beseecheth'

that West be forced to cough up. Probably he did; the endorsement on the petition sounds short-tempered: 'The High Court of Admirality is required to take such order in this cause, that the Boarde be no more troubled.'

Being the widow of an admiral and a titled man did not protect a woman against the same worries and degradations that drove her untitled sisters.

'The humble petition of the Lady Button, declaring to His Matie ye ffourty yeares service of her late husband Sir Thomas Button, and ye distress'd state of herselfe and children who have nothinge left for their mayntenance, but some parte of his wages that was due unto him in ye Navy.'

She also indicates a long ordeal:

'Now in respect her poore estate hath binne made more miserable by her long attendance upon this suite, who hath already spent a whole yeare since her husbands death and pre-vayled nothinge therein.'

The delay has been caused by a difference over the length of time that her husband served. In telling this, she throws interesting light on a higher officer's pay.

'Whereas Y° Maties Officers have certified her husbands realle [actual] attendance to have binne but 928 daies, [I beg] that Y° will allow him the full tyme, 1551 daies at that day of his death, seeing he was never absent from his charge,'
except at the Admiralty's own orders. The sum she petitions for would be a great consideration, if obtained:

'That Y° Matie wilbe pleased to graunt ye warrant for his paye at twentie shillings a day as he hath always binne paid as Admirall. And in respect [considering] that Captains have had 10 shillings and 13/4d perdiem, allowed in lesser Shipps than her husband served in.'

She begs 'speedie reliefe of her most miserable and distress'd estate', incidentally revealing that Sir Thomas left his affairs in bad shape: 'his whole estate being legally solde for paiement of his debts, yet divers of ye Credittors still unsatisfied'.

The next petition, by a strange chance, brushed against one of the famous assassinations of history. Isabell Musgrave, with two little children, was left 'the distress'd widdowe of Lieutenant ffrancis Musgrave, hee having valliantlie loste his life on the fourlourne hope' at Retz. She petitioned the Duke of Buckingham,

Lord High Admiral, for £50 due of her husband's pay. 'All which the Duke took into his noble consideracon, and promised to be a meanes [to use his influence].' By an unlucky chance he was just going to Portsmouth, so Isabell had to follow him there. 'His grace havinge a warrant readie for that purpose [payment of the £50] and shee at great charge there attendinge; but by his graces ontimelie death, shee is left to her former distresses.'

The untimely death was his murder (September, 1628) by John Felton. 'The Duke fell down dead in the hall, with much effusion of blood.' His wife was still in bed, upstairs; her lady-in-waiting heard some sort of commotion and casually stepped outside to investigate. 'The Lady Anglesea, lookinge down into the hall, went immediately with a cry into the Duchess's chamber, and there fell down on the floor.' This was the announcement, to Katherine, of her husband's death. Of course to Isabell it only meant that she had had her long expensive journey for nothing, with the money snatched away just as she was about to get it, and that she would have to start the machinery of petition all over again. But this is one of the stories that may be followed through completely, that tells how Isabell was in the end luckier than most, and even adds—later on—the bonus of an unpredictable conclusion.

Occasionally, beside this lamentation of wives, other sad voices are heard:

The humble petition of Joyce Cresset Sheweth that y° pet^r sonne Thomas Cresset was three yeares went Chirurgeon's [Surgeon's] Mate in his Matie Shipp the Sea Horse and was to receive for his pay, twenty shillings a Moneth, as by his Tiquet [pay-ticket] appeareth. And y° pet^r sonne hath since departed this life, leaving y° pet^r in great misery and distresse, hee beinge the onely staffe of her old age.

[Her] humble suite therefore is, that y° Lo^{pps} out of your noble disposicons would give order that shee, being a poore aged woman, may receive all such moneys as were due him for the said voyage.

Attached to this petition are the certificate of Thomas's service

and of his death, also his will. He commits his soul to God and
his body to the sea or the earth, 'as it shall happen', and
continues: 'My will and mynde is, if it shall please God to take
mee out of this miserable world, that my pay bee paid to
my louvinge mother Joyce Cresset for her reliefe and comfort in
her declyninge and aged yeares.' A good son, Thomas, and the
endorsement on the petition, to the Treasurer of the Navy, is
hopeful.

This next petition is irresistible not so much for its matter—
though even that is interesting—but because it stands unequalled
in the Papers merely as dialect. By a dazzlement of phonetics this
speech comes to us as from living mouths; the petitioner rejoices
in the name of Ewfame Lookup, and Ewfame [Euphemia]
addresses the King with special confidence, as his countrywoman.

'Most sacred Soveraine,' she begins, rather unusually, 'this
petition be [by] Ewfame Lookup the relict of single [one]
David Gardner, Shipper in Leith, and her sax fatherles childrene;
that her said single husband being quereta [quarter] owner of
the Shipp callit the Gift of God departed this Lyfe in anno 1623,
and left nothing for his said relict and childrene bot the quereta of
the said Shipp, estimat to be worth twentie fowre thousand merkes
Scotts money. And the Shipp being pressed for Y° Maties wares
[wars] against Dunkirk, was throw stres of wedder [through
stress of weather] Cast away; to the bitter robyne of the poore
widowe and of her onlie meanes and moyen for the sustentation
and educann of her childrene; she doth humiblie beseech your
ma^{tie} for gode cawz [good cause] seing yow are the fathere of the
fatherles and husband of the widowe, to comiserat her miserable
estate, as shall seeme meete to Y° gratious plesour.'

Euphemia's plea has special weight because her husband's ship
had been pressed—as was very frequent—for war service. Her
first petition, from Edinburgh, is rather grandly attested by six
of the 'Councill of Scotland': Kinghorn, Southesk, Marischal,
Mar, etc. A later copy, spelled in more rampant Scots, shows that
her trust was not misplaced; King James by his own endorsement
responds cozily to these familiar sounds: 'His ma^{tie} is gratiously
pleased to recomend this petitione to the hon^{bles} off the Admiraltie

c

of England for the competent [adequate] satisfaction.' With such a recommendation, of course Euphemia got her warrant for payment; whether she could collect on it is another matter, all departments under slovenly James being short of cash. But we are in her debt merely for knowing that she was called Ewfame, let alone for this legacy of daily talk as heard, *circa* 1623, in the seaport of Leith.

'Reliefe'

1600—1700

The help entreated by these multitudes of distracted women, balanced with their children on the very razor-edges of destitution, did not exist in any organized form such as regular allowances from governmental or Naval funds reserved for the purpose. Some well-intentioned plans, to be noted, shared a common fate: no sooner formulated than forgotten. During almost every English reign up to the nineteenth century a chronic lack of money was the normal condition, often amounting to a sort of unacknowledged bankruptcy; expensive wars left little margin for expensive compassion.

Yet this is not to say that petitions went unseen, or were ignored. Considering the sheer mass of these appeals that never stopped coming, considering the unnerving clamour from them that never stopped rending the air, the Council coped manfully and—it seems—never tried to evade the fearsome problem by a blanket exclusion of all such matter from their meetings, or a policy of mass-refusal. They really examined each document, reviewed the circumstances, and did what they could.

What they could do, however, amounted to painfully little. On the great majority of petitions are noted small sums given, on the average from £10 to £50, depending on the deceased husband's rank. These pittances were often the end result of months of supplication and waiting, and even considering the then-value of money, how far would £10 carry a woman with three or four small children? And having secured this relief, she could not petition again.

Yet the Papers carry some examples of yearly pensions for the seaman's widow, and their rarity makes them all the more interesting. Judith Newman's petition, when first submitted (1632) gives no inkling of what it led to:

Late wife [*sic*] of Richard Newman deceased Humblie sheweth: that Y° Pet^r said husband was 32 yeares Chiefe Clerke to the Comissioners of Y° Matie royall Navie. And did faithfullie and suffitientlie ynforme [fill] the Service, [but] left ye pet^r in verie poore estate.

She now tells why:

'The reason is, because he had a place of credebt [credit], hee spente the meanes he gott in the Countenancinge thereof.'

In other words, they spent every penny he made keeping up the appearances they judged proper to his important position. For this reason

'hee left ye pet^r and five children altogether unprovided for, whoe in his time lived in plentie, and now in this harde time doe heavilie suffer.'

Judith now asks for something unusual, but the very fact of her asking it shows that it was not altogether unknown:

'The premises considered, shee most humblie beseecheth Y° Matie to graunte her some yearlie reliefe to be paid by the Trer [Treasurer] of the Navye, [in] such aproporcon [proportion] as Y° Matie shall thincke meete.'

Attached are two endorsements: the Navy Commissioners' certificate of her husband's service, and an attestation of her present poverty.

Judith's uncommon request stirred the Council to an uncommon proceeding: (December 22, 1635)

'Wee desire the Officers of the Navy to send us some Presidente [precedent], if ye like Allowance hath att any time bin given in the Navy.'

Thus prodded, the Navy Office set to and actually dug up something from the years of the Armada:

'Divers of ye *Revenge* men after ye ship was lost in a fight with the Spaniard, had pencons of 8d pr diem during their lives: grtd [granted] by Queene Eliz: paid out of ye Chechque.' [Treasury.]

The brilliant fellows even found a more recent instance under James I, but by word of mouth, not written record.

'Wee are likewise crediblie informed, that one Mrs Johnson an Engineers widdowe had a pencon of 100 merke p. annum grtd by his Mat^ie and paide out of the Office of Ordnance. But, wee have had no presidents in our tymes, of any pencons paid in ye Office of ye Navy.'

But for all the lack of precedents, they advise stretching a point.

'Yet knowing the honesty dilligence and good service of this poore woman's husband in his life time, and that shee hath a charge of 5 small children on her hands and is no way able to maintayne them: Wee therefore humblie recomend her lamentable case, for to be relieved by his Mat^ie as in [his] wisdome shall seeme goode.'

The last endorsement carries the joyful news:

'Wee have thought fitt to certifie, that ninepence p. diem wilbe in our opinions a reasonable allowance toward her reliefe, and her five children left to her charge.'

This would be the equivalent of about 40p. or one dollar a day. In the end it transpires that her husband was drowned in 1624,

that this is 1632, and that during the eight years between King
Charles has been paying her an allowance out of his own pocket
—by many testimonies in the Papers, the sort of thing he did
continually. By the way, Council's bloodhounds, while scenting
out precedents, missed one of only sixteen years before: 'Letters
Patent for relief of Amy Lynstead widdowe of William, and
Joane, wife of Ribert Morse, seamen.' Lynstead had been killed
by Turks and Morse was in captivity. But relief *by Letters Patent*,
for wives of common seamen at that, is an astounding anomaly;
no trace of even this one example survives, except as an entry in
a Register of Warrants.

Yet, beside the petition for a money grant, there did exist
other twists and dodges for defeating starvation—thought up by
ingenious women, with hungry children to quicken their
wits. A demonstration of this (March, 1628) begins with the same
old story: Katherine Warde, widow, petitions the Duke of
Buckingham for herself and her young family; her husband's
ship, the *Hector* of Dover, 'was lost in his Mat^ie service, by which
shee is lefte much in debte and destitute of means', her statement
being attested by 'the hand and seale of the Maior of the said
countrie'. Katherine then makes her request, but not for direct
financial aid:

'Shee humblie beseecheth Y° Grace to graunt unto her, the
oulde prize [captured] shipp called the *James* of Bourage [Bruges?]
with her Tacklyn [tackle] beinge all of small value, as Sir John
Hipisley can informe Y° Grace.'

Obviously Admiral Hippisley was at least an acquaintance, and
she had consulted him on the propriety of asking for the ship.
Upon her petition is Buckingham's endorsement in his own hand:
'I desire Sir Jo: Hippesley B^t to take this peticon into Consideration, and to signify in wrighting his opinion thereof, what ye
ship desired is worth, *and whether she be adjudged his Maties, or noe.*'

The italicised words are important: sometimes the Admiralty
Court pronounced the capture illegal, and returned the ship to
its original owners. Probably Katherine was successful; when a

petition got as high as the King or the Lord High Admiral its chances were good, though the Papers do not record the whole story.

We have better luck with the case of Isabell Musgrave. It may be remembered that we left Isabell disconsolate at Portsmouth, her hopes of her husband's back wages blasted by Buckingham's murder. On returning to London, she petitioned the King direct for the fifty pounds. The document no longer exists, but this time the blank is filled by Isabell's own allusions in a second petition to the King: 'Shee revived her suite to Y⁰ Matie, whose answere was, Y⁰ would not graunte any more of that kind (i.e., cash payments).' But Charles, in his way invincibly compassionate toward the poor and struggling, had qualified his refusal by telling Isabell 'that if shee would finde any other befitting suite (suitable application), he would graunte it her'. And Isabell, brave pertinaceous woman, has done exactly that:

'Nowe, shee havinge found an ould prize shipp called the St. Peter of Callis [Calais], certified to bee no waye fitt for Y⁰ Matie service, and praysed [appraised] but att £24 att the highest raite, shee humblie therefore beseecheth Y⁰ Matie to graunt unto her the said vessell, to comforte her and her children.'

Isabell got quick action on this; the endorsement (November, 1628) shows that the whole procedure took about a month. 'My Lord Steward sent word to prepare a warrant to draw upp a graunt of ye prize shipp herein mentioned, for ye petitioner.'

The Navy Office acknowledges the order:

'Wee his Maties Commissioners for sale of prize Shipps and goodes, have received a Privy Seale, requiring us to make present [immediate] delivery of the St. Peter, with all her takle [ropes, anchors, etc.] unto Mrs Isabell Musgrave widdow, as a free guift unto her from his Matie. The which wee are ready to obey and deliver the said Shipp with all her takle. And humbly remaine . . . (Three signatures).

But all is not as peaceful in Eden as it seems: a querulous serpent raises his voice, and in another petition goes over the heads of the Commissioners and addresses a more exalted authority: 'To the Lords of his Maties Privy Councill, the humble petition of George Burridge Maryiner':

Burridge goes on to tell how, 'going forth Master of the 5th Whelpe, hee took the Shipp called the Sainte Peter of Callis and sente her in, as prize. Further sheweth that there was an Order made at this honoble board *for an allowance to the Man bringine in Such prize, the beste Cable and the beste Anchor in any such shipp got, by him taken*'.

Having reminded Council of their own ruling on this point, he ventilates his grievance: he has been at sea on the King's service, and has only just got back to hear the disgusting intelligence:

'And nowe the said Shipp being latelie given awaye to one Isabell Musgrave, *and shee beinge to receive for the same*, £380:

His humble suite nowe is that Y° Lo^pps wilbe pleased to order, that the said Isabell shall give Y° Pet^r full satisfacion for the said Anchor and Cable, beinge his right by the said Order, as not belonginge to her Guifte.'

Whether Burridge got his anchor and cable away from Isabell, we never find out. But this is a minor point compared to what followed—the uproar of protest from a department hitherto silent. In fact, Isabell and her prize may even have touched off the commotion; or at least some inquiry might be expected as to who had appraised, at £24, a ship that was sold for £380. But whether or not Isabell's case impelled the steel, a howl was set up that revealed a corner full of inconspicuous little grafts involving prize ships, that had been going on merrily for some time.

These prizes taken at sea were the starry-eyed hope of all seamen of every rank, since all aboard the captor shared, at least theoretically, in the spoils. Captains were alert to pounce on ships of any hostile nation, and—England frequently being at war with someone—there were always plenty of eligible candidates.

These ships seem to have been mostly in the small-size range and varied greatly in value, state of repair, and whatever. Once captured and the cargo removed, appraised and sold—after innumerable squabbles, pilferings and contending claims in the Court of Admiralty—the ship herself was handed over to an office called the Commissioners for the sale of Prize Ships. Here the rot began, in a literal sense.

Even before Isabell got her ship there had been some faint notes of unease from these Prize Ship officials, who on their own showing had little or no authority. More than anything else they were assessors and auctioneers, merely reporting on what they could get for ships. That these sums were often ludicrously small was not their fault, they pointed out; prize ships were too often allowed to deteriorate 'by lying long undisposed of'. They quoted the *Wind Hound* and the *Little Saint Peter* from many such examples, which after inexplicable delays had had to go for what they would fetch. Meanwhile matters were thickening up, and exactly six months after Isabell got her ship, they came to the boil in a letter from the Prize Ship Office to the Lords of Admiralty. This letter displays not only protest, but every symptom of indignation long suppressed.

This game of prize ships, they tell the Lords, in effect, has gone on long enough. Captured ships have begun to constitute in themselves a sort of currency: seamen's widows got them frequently and this was not so bad, but improper persons also managed to secure ownership at nominal or derisory prices by means 'of having them disvalued'. Under-assessment meant dirty work somewhere—Isabell's ship being a flagrant example—but by existing regulations the Prize Ship Commissioners could do nothing about it. Therefore they petitioned the Admiralty for increased powers so that they could deal with such abuses, and incidentally (they claim) prevent the stealing from the ship of sails, ropes, bolts, or any other object that could be picked up or unscrewed.

How much good the Commissioners' protest did them might be mentioned now, to dispose of the subject. Eight years later (July, 1637) the Admiralty inquired for the money proceeding

from the sale of a captured Turkish frigate, and got the disheartening news that 'the friggate was sold by the candle[1] to William
Bowles marriner for £10-15-0, beinge the moste that was bidden
for her'. Again the Admiralty ask for the proceeds of two ships.
The Prize Ship Office replies with the even worse news that the
ships in question are old wrecks not worth repairing, and snuffles
disconsolately, 'Wee present their true state, for Y° hon^ble consideration'. But the least thought about Isabell's transaction points
it up for what it is—starkly and glaringly a racket. How could
the petitioning widow even know that a certain ship was coming
under the hammer, unless some friend in the Prize Ship Office
tipped her off and arranged a false valuation for her benefit? Most
likely, also, the petitioner had never set eyes on what she was
bidding for, since the ship would be moored at some port more
or less distant. But by the testimony of the Prize Office itself, as
well as of petitions like Isabell's, captured ships were a sort of
recognized form of relief for seamen's widows—not the common
seaman's, but only the widows of officers, and various attempts
had been made to stiffen up the procedure even in these cases. For
example, Isabell cites the requirement that she must 'obteyne a
sufficient man' to vouch for her, preferably 'a Barronett'; but
Katherine Warde's petition carries nothing of the kind, and
obviously the most direct route toward getting a ship was a friend
in the Prize Ship Office.

Another class of wifely petition appears in the Papers with
moderate frequency, whose application is not so much for a
dole as for compensation. These are the widows of merchants who
were either owners or part-owners of cargo ships. Such ships
were too often 'pressed' [impressed] into Navy service as fighting
ships, a change of pace likely to do them little good in the long
run. One such story is told in January, 1628, by Francis Brook, a
son petitioning on behalf of his mother; the ship referred to had
belonged to her deceased husband. Brook begins by apologizing
pitifully: 'Let mee not bee too teadious to Y° Hon^r, but I would
move Y° concerninge the Moneys due to my poore Mother, for
the Shipp taken [impressed] by Sir James Bagge at Plymouth.'

[1] At auction. While the stump of a candle burned, bids could be made.

C*

This unfortunate vessel had been employed as a fire-ship and completely destroyed. But some time previous to the petition, Brook had received good news: that Kenrick Edisbury, Navy Surveyor, had left 'restinge here in one of the Townesmens hands, £300' as partial payment of Mrs Brook's claim.

So far so good, but now a discordant note—the old bitter tale of unscrupulous hands entrusted with other people's property, with no intention of giving it up. By Francis's allusions it is clear that the money has been asked for again and again, without result. 'If there might bee *any* way to procure payment of yt', he concludes despairingly, 'Y° hon^r should doe a most charitable worke in ye releevinge of a truly poore widow and manie children.' The wresting of his mother's money from the hands of the cheat—the £300 was worth at least £3,000 in modern currency— meant for her family, literally, the difference between life and death. But this variety of fraud pales before a more terrible petition, fortunately rare—but not rare enough—whose ugliness is of the nethermost pit:

'Mary Blundell the distress'd wife of Richard Blundell Captive in Argiers [Algiers]: hee was bought and put in a galley and continueth in miserable slavery wherein his owner doth keepe him in cheynes in the gallies hold.'

Mary meanwhile has been begging and scraping for money to pay her husband's ransom, joining with other wives in a 'generall collection, which money was paid to Captain Leat. And yett,' she continues desolately, 'the poore Captives continew in misery and bondage, and have had noe benefit by the Collection'.

In other words Leat had put the ransom money in his own pocket, and Mary continues with heroic restraint, 'Y° poore Pet^r doth therefore most humblye beseeche Y° Lo^pps, that Y° will bee pleased to call the said Captain Leat to accompt, how he hath bestowed that Collection, and that Y° Pet^rs poore captivated (*sic*) husband may have his share in the Collection, towarde his ransome'.

A note on the petition indicates that the matter was to be looked into, and there the story ends. However, a curious item floats to the surface about a year later, from which conclusions are permissible. One Leat is named as a principal in a considerable warehouse robbery involving 'currants and figgs'. In the charge he is no longer called Captain but Mr Leat, and there could hardly be two Nicholas Leats. The fact of his participation in the robbery indicates him as capable of the peculiarly scabrous theft of the ransom money, and the loss of his title may also indicate that Council looked at him closely enough to throw him out of the Service.

Last of all, when the bitter fight to cling to her place on the social ladder has been lost inch by inch, comes

The humble peticon of Elizabeth Tralfall a poore distress'd widow

Most humbly sheweth That y^r pet^r late husband deceased, rob'd of his whole estate by Pirates and soe utterly undon and dying suddenly thereafter in extreame want

In tender comiseracon of which y^o poore supp^t doth most humbly beseech Y^r sacred Matie to graunt unto her y^r gracious letters pattente for the Collection of the benevolence of good people, for the comfort of Y^o supp^t and her 5 children

In other words, an application for a licence to beg; last, lost cry from a darkness of final defeat.

The whole wretched bundle may be tied up with strings of fraying nerves—of officials who could no longer endure the perpetual sight and sound of hungry women and children: the Navy Commissioners urgently beg the Council to relieve them of that part of their business which concerns needy wives, or widows of seamen 'slayne in the Service'. First of all, they have no time for it; secondly, 'it is a great disservice to have the lamentable cries of such persons in the eares of seamen, who by multitudes have recourse to our office'. Well-founded apprehensions—that all those poor shrill creatures, perpetually underfoot, could supply, to the seaman, too vivid a picture of what might become of his own wife and children.

Resourceful Wives

By contrast with the stylized keening of the wife in penury, with her single note of paralyzing helplessness and fear, other types of women's petitions came like a breath of fresh air. This second class of women were in scarcely less trouble than the first— confronted either with serious money losses or the imminent loss of livelihood—but they were able to face these troubles with considerable energy and courage because they had qualifications foreign to the great majority of their female contemporaries. For this reason they speak in a quite different voice from that of the woman without a trade or profession and distracted by the thought of her hungry children, and this voice is wonderfully interesting. Also, whereas our first variety of petitioner might be either widow or wife (of a Barbary captive or seaman long-absent on voyage) these women of the second class possess one similarity in common: all of them, without exception, are widows. For unless this misfortune had overtaken them, we should not have heard their voices at all.

The most attractive and enterprising of these widows—the cream of the crop one might say—had been wives of purveyors and suppliers to the Navy. On their husbands' death, they now petition for a continuation of his existing contracts, claiming experience and capability and asking no more than to be allowed to compete in the business world of men, on men's terms. One such petition is among undated Papers for 1623; in it Mrs Ann Johnson represents the demise of her husband, formerly a brewer to the Navy. 'Shee having helped him verie much during his lyfetime, and onderstandinge that businesse verie well', asks that she may continue to supply the Navy with beer on the same terms, without bringing in the arguments of poverty and a young family.

Women like Mrs Johnson charmingly illustrate not only the nature of their business relations with the Navy, but also the diversity of their trades. A Mrs Venner was the contracting supplier, 'alone', of flags to the Navy. From 1626 to 1649 she enjoyed the monopoly of this highly skilled business, in which she translated the drawings of Engravers to the Mint into fabric. Unfortunately the warrant of her appointment is elusive, but we have an order of the kind she had to fill: 'Three Standards, a vice adm^{ll} and rere adm^{ll} three fflags apiece, with two Jackes for every shipp in the ffleet. Of Ensignes and pendents many are wanting, which may bee no longer delayed.' The irritable conclusion is not addressed to Mrs Venner for tardiness in supplying the flags, but to the Navy Commissioners for not ordering them in time.

'Katherine Byworth, widdow' was in the business of cartage, now called haulage, but of one commodity only—ammunition for the Navy. She might have remained forever unknown to us, if not for the difficult situation—shared by innumerable of her contemporaries under the Commonwealth—in which she found herself. The Navy had been a special victim of the great despoiler Cromwell, and Katherine had to make strenuous efforts to get what it owed her:

'That whereas there is due to Y^o Pet^r for her servants [employees], horses and carts imployed in Drawing of Ammunition for ye Service of ye ffleete, by a Debenter [Debenture] signed by ye Officers of Ordnance, in all amounting to the Sume One hundred eighty seaven Pounds ten shillings and ten pence. Y^o Pet^r hath not received any part of them, by which shee is disabled to pay her servants and other Creditors, and cannot subsist unless Y^o please to graunt order, that shee may be paid forthwith.'

We are also privileged to meet Mrs Russell, because in 1660 she submitted quotations for various commodities, apparently by request:

ffine Holland Twine	at	11d
Blacking	at	9$\frac{1}{2}$s pr Barr
Glew	at	2s
Good Trayne Oyl	at	2s Gall
Charcoale	at	13s Bush
Broomes	at	12s Doz

The list carries a first endorsement: *Mrs Russell's lowest price of some provisions she hath in her hands*, and on a second list a second endorsement shows that the Navy Office beat her down even on 'her lowest price', and on some items (not all) she did make a reduction; they note smugly, *Mrs Russells prices, upon our abatement*.

These four women representing, in small cross-section, so wide a diversity of trades as brewing, flag-making, haulage and ship's-chandlering, were lucky ones who inherited going concerns from their husbands. Among others, not so lucky, were brave resource-ful souls who instead of sitting down in the ruins and wailing, turned to and got busy in a number of directions unexpected in nature as in scope. Alice Murray, a seaman's widow, set up in second-hand clothes; it is rather remarkable that she travelled regularly to the Low Countries to replenish her stocks. Why? because of the pre-eminence of Flemish fabrics? or because there existed in Brussels or Bruges a large flea-market to which thieves or disbanded soldiers brought their loot of rich garments either stolen or stripped off the dead on battlefields? Whatever the reason, Alice periodically took cargo of one sort to the Low Countries and brought back a mass of used finery until the 'Protectorate' began to clamp restriction after restriction on people journeying out of England. This brought about a first refusal to give Alice the necessary pass for overseas travel. Desperate, she appealed to some unspecified board, and was lucky enough to find on it sensible and reasonable men willing to speak up for her. This gave rise to the following curious petition—not from Alice personally, but from others in her behalf:

'Alice Murray, a poore woman, who hath to our knowledg had some poore tradings out of England into the Low Countries for old apprel [apparel] and such like odd and overwore trifles, her credett not reaching for much [her dealings not amounting to much], with which she hath made a poore living for herselfe and three poore children, ever since her husband dyed, and never yett denyed to pass [refused a pass] before this tyme. And ye pore Pet^r hath already shipped her goods, being of small value, and she hourly expects the shipp shall set to sea, and in case she be restrayned from goinge, it will be the utter undoinge of her and her said children.'

Her sponsors now deal with the suspicion that she is trying to flee England permanently, like so many others during the 'Protectorate'.

'She saith that shee hath noe means to stay beyond the Seas, which wee believe: shee having a house neere Moorsgate London. All which wee have thought good to certify in behalf of that poore distressed Woman.'

No clue survives, apparently, as to the petition's success or non-success. The episode does, however, suggest a quibble: could Alice's business be quite so small as represented, in view of her frequent and expensive journeys abroad?

Mary Keynes was another brave woman who knew the full weight of poverty and lonely fear, but refused to go under without a fight. 'Y^o Pet^r hath bine left in much want, with 4 small children and noe means to relieve them.' Mary, however, was not entirely without someone to care whether she lived or died.

'Her brother Edward Eldrington hath sent to Y^o Pet^r for the reliefe of herselfe and Children, eight hoggsheads of Bermodos Tobaccoe, which nowe remayneth in the Custome House, and shee is no ways able to pay Custome or any parte thereof, in respect of her great wante.

'May it therefor please Y^o Hon^{rs}, of Y^o Noble consideracon, to give order that the said tobaccoe, beinge of very small value, may be delivered unto Y^o Pet^r without payinge any Custome, towardes the support of her Family which are otherwise lik to perish.'

No endorsement; we never have the comfort of knowing whether Mary retrieved and sold the little shipment and, to that extent, staved off the menacing tomorrow.

If 'doughty' is not an adjective generally applied to women, all the same Mary Page makes a powerful bid for it. Mary, judging by the documents that follow, had the soul of a pirate, the eye of a businessman, a steel-trap opportunism, and the ability to gauge the favourable moment. In her case the favourable moment was England's state of war with the Dutch, the French and assorted lesser enemies, and she seized it by petitioning for—and getting— a document in small demand among ladies, or so one might think.

[Undated] 'A Letter of Marque being graunted (according to an ordinance of Parlia^t) unto Mary Page widdow; shee and company sett forth a ship called ye *Mary*: her Comission was to Seize on Dutch, ffrench or other shipps of ye enemys of this Comon-Wealth.'

Mary certainly appears as the leader of this enterprise; whether she financed it or merely contributed the ship—property inherited from her husband—never appears. Whatever the case, 'shee and company' meant business.

'Shee seized a shipp called ye *Surmy*: at ye time of ye Seizure, their [*sic*] was noe court of Admiralty: And ye Master of ye *Surmy* who pretended himselfe to be of Lisbon, petitioned ye hon^{ble} Councill of State for releasement.'

But Mary was ready for him; she had searched his ship and found 'writinges' (enemy dispatches? Royalist correspondence?). These she offered in evidence before the Council; shortly afterward the Admiralty Court got under way again.

'And then ye Judges beinge apointed, Mary Page began her Loyall course for condemning of ye said shipp and goodes.'

The 'writinges' she found aboard the *Surmy* were good enough for the judges, 'who condemned ye Shipp for Lawfull prize'. It is true that this is not quite the end of the story; 'ye Claymers of ye *Surmy* appealed from ye Sentence'. The appeal could not be ignored; by a jotting on the document three commissioners [named] and some 'doctors of ye Civill-Law' [unnamed] are

'Humbly prayed to be pleased to spend some few houres one afternoone at Sergents-Inne, to hear the Cause, and to give a Diffinitive Judgment'.

Here the Papers, as frequently, break off the narrative; where the judgment should be, the page is blank. But by the languid and unspecific tone of the appointment—'some few houres one afternoone'—it seems fairly clear that 'shee and company' were going to hang on to what they had captured. Mary was certainly in her ship when the *Surmy* was taken; the lovely thought that 'shee' in person commanded her legalized pirates, remains a matter of pleasant speculation.

A final section of widows of character whose troubles had to do with the Navy emerges from large financial backgrounds, and to that extent were more productive of cares and complications. These were the widows of men who, as well as commanding ships of merchant-importers under Naval convoy, were also part-owners of the cargo, an arrangement by no means uncommon. Such women, on their husbands' death, had to grapple alone with problems involving important sums of money. The first petition of this sort arises from the breach of a Naval treaty between the English and the Dutch; the able presentation of rather complicated facts is noteworthy.

The humble petition of Elizabeth Salmon widdow, relict of Captain Robert Bonner:

'Sheweth that ye pet^r husband was capt. of the shipp called the *Dragon* and had under his Comaund two other Shipps called the *Lyon* and the *Expedition*, which shipps was trading in the East Indyes, richly laden with merchantable goods

'*That Articles of Peace as to trade with the East Indyes being concluded 1st June 1651, between the United Provinces and this Comonwealth*, and the English Fleet expecting nothing but freindship from the Dutch: [nevertheless] on the 1st October, severall Dutch shipps treacherously fell upon the said shipp called the *Dragon*, then lying at ancor, and killed not only ye pet^r said Husband (useing him most barbarously after he was mortally wounded) but also most of his men. And tooke the said Shipp and lading to the value of £100,000 in which ye Pet^r said Husband had a share to the value of £7000 at the least, and Y^o Pet^r was left a disconsolate Widdow and her children fatherlesse and spoyled [dispoiled] of all their means of subsistence

[Therefore she prays] 'that reparacon may be demaunded of them for the high iniury done, and satisfaccon for the death of her said husband and the losse of his estate.'

The endorsement on this is again out of the ordinary: *Ffriday next, some of the East India Companie to attend this Committee.* The Salmons had been people of substance, and something had to be done. The Council's second endorsement on the same petition reads: *That the peticon of Mrs Salmon bee referred to the consideracon of the Comittee for forreigne affairs.* This sounds suspiciously like the run-around, but not hopelessly so; the Commonwealth would presumably try to protect people of such extensive mercantile interests, or at least not let the matter drag until it fell into limbo.

Happy endings have been scarce enough in these examples; but if one note of triumph can be sounded, we owe it to Mary Thompson. Her case, metaphorically touching Naval affairs on their outer shores, by a coincidence touches Mary on *her* outer shores—literally. In the piecemeal narrative of the Papers, all the ins and outs of the affair gradually reveal not only themselves but the formidable silhouette of Mary, a widow who knew exactly how to take care of herself—and with the full weight of the Navy Board and the Admiralty Courts against her.

When the Papers begin the story in June, 1630, something important had already happened; an Amsterdam ship called the *St Peter of Horne* with 'her wholl lading of Deale boards Masts and other goods, was lately driven ashore by contrary wynds and Tempest, nere Arundell in the Country of Sussex'. This first document of a series goes on to state that 'certeyne Masts, part of the said lading, were bought by the Officers of the Navy, for his Matie service. Which said Masts are remayning on the grounds of one Mrs Thompson'. Here Mary makes her first appearance as owner of a sea-coast property on which the masts had come ashore—perhaps jettisoned to save the ship, though this is nowhere stated. The Admiralty now demands the surrender of the masts, and appoints agents to get them. 'Wee doe hereby authorise and require you, and the Justices of the Peace next adjoyning the said place, that you forthwith cause the said Masts to be delivered to you who are appointed to receave the same. Nether you nor any of you may fayle herein', the warrant ends ominously, 'as you will annsweare the contrary att your p'ille [peril].'

A month or so passes, when a letter appears (July, 1630), referring to them on a much more urgent note. 'There being great want of Mastes for supplye of his Matie Shippinge', it announces, 'wee have given order to transport the same to Portsmouth.'

Not if Mary knew it, however.

'But the said Mastes are halled [held] by one Mrs. Mary Thompson a widdowe on her own grounde, where she deteyneth them, pretendinge a right to them as wrecke, not permitting anie to take them off her grounde, *notwithstanding a decree in the Admiraltie* [Court], adjuidinge [adjudging] them noe wrecke.'

But Mary was not in the least interested in the Admiralty's definition of wrecks, as 'severall gentlemen of the Comission' quickly found out; not only did she refuse to let them come on her land to take away the masts, 'but on the contrarye used scornefull and reproachfull speeches (whereof this Bearer can more pticularly informe you). Wee therefore request a warrant comaundinge her to answere her contempt. And that,' they specify, 'with as much speede as maie bee, in regard of the important occasion of his Matie service.'

'This Bearer' was one Thomas Batten, who now proceeds to recount their first man-handling by Mary.

'Wee went to Mrs Mary Thompson to demaund the Masts, and shewed her the Letter of Assistance. Her answere was, shee could shew us as good as that. And told us the Masts were hers, and wee should not have them, and that she had sould them, and would avouch [stand by] the sale. Wee told her shee would bring herselfe into a greate deale of trouble; her answere was that shee had a great desire to see Y° Lo^pps [of Admiralty] and many such like speeches.'

After this first repulse by Mary, the Commission tottered off in search of aid and comfort.

'Then went wee to the two next [nearest] Justices, who sent for her to perswade her, but shee was still the same woman.'

Mary the same woman was bad news enough for the Commission, but one of the Justices had even worse.

'Mr Higgins told us that shee might bring an Action for Trespas for comeing on her Land, and told us the Letter of Assistance would not helpe us in it.' But then again, rather feebly half-reversing himself, Mr Higgins advised the Commission to put Mary to the test—that is, make a determined effort to get the masts, 'and see if shee would withstande us'. In what can only be felt as a rash moment, they took this advice.

'The next day wee got eight or tenn men with shovells to digg them out of ye single [shingle]. But shee was there ready with her Tennants, being three of them with Staves and Pitchforks, and told us wee should not touch a Mast there, and that shee would indict us for coming on her land. Soe', peeps William, obviously a broken reed, 'wee went noe further in the matter.'

The wars were far from over, however; it was Mary who, without losing a moment, invaded the enemy camp by going direct to the Privy Council 'July 9, 1630, att Whytehall' only three days after leading her pitchfork militia to such good effect. Her petition continues to exhibit her knowledge of law that enabled her to take such a high tone with the Commission, and conveys the voice of a landed proprietor whose ground of utterance is quite different from mercantile people's, however wealthy. First of all Mary, identifying herself as 'Guardian of her daughter Katherine Tompson',[1] deliberately subordinates her own right to the right of her daughter who will inherit.

She then goes on to recount how 'there was driven on shore upon the Lands of the said Katherine, 28 Masts for Shipps, in or about the moneth of October 1628'—surprisingly, almost two years before. Another surprise is that Mary has already been in court over these masts, also two years ago; the owner of the wrecked ship, Jacob Kast of Amsterdam, 'did implead [sue]

[1] Mary spelled her own name in two or three different ways.

Y^r Suppliant in the Admiralty Court for recovery of the said
Masts. And in respect hee offered no proofe, nor gave any Libell
[bills of lading, etc.] of his clayme for a wholl yeare and upwards,
the cause was thereupon dismissed by that Court.' But notwithstanding that the masts had been confirmed as Mary's property,
Jacob refused to give up, getting various warrants and letters of
restitution from the Admiralty Court, which Mary itemizes with
withering scorn. Then she reveals the ace up her sleeve; this is
what she meant when, on the Commission's flourishing the
Letter of Assistance at her, she had retorted, 'I can show you as
good as that'. The 'good as that' was a warrant in her possession
awarding her any flotsam cast up on her property '*by graunt of
Queen Elizabeth*, which graunt ever since shee and her predecessors
have practised and enjoyed', a big gun indeed. Now a speculative
digression, very brief, on the validity of this warrant.

Technically, on a new sovereign succeeding, the warrants of the
deceased sovereign became mostly null and void. Mary's warrant
may have belonged to this class. But it is reasonable to suppose,
by many references, that though Elizabeth had died some thirty
years ago, a peculiar veneration and power still clung to her
legend. This cherishing of her memory may have derived in part
from the fact that James I had been no very impressive heir, and
that Charles I was not yet a distinct image on the public conscious-
ness. But Elizabeth—Elizabeth was a different story; thousands
of people still alive remembered her and loved her, had even
served under her, and her lingering, mysterious aura of prestige
was not to be ignored. So Mary, in producing Elizabeth's attestation of her right, boldly challenged the Admiralty judges to
declare the great Queen's warrant worthless, which was certainly
putting them in a cleft stick, to say nothing of a delicate position.

Having done this, Mary's petition takes a conciliatory turn.
First she defines her own money position as none too good: 'the
said Masts have caused great breaches [damage] to the seaworkes
of her Land in divers places, whereby shee hath been much damnifyed [out of pocket].

'Her most humble sute therefore is, that shee may enjoy the
benefitt of the said Masts. Or,' she adds, 'if his Matie Navy have

occasion to use them, that shee may have reasonable allowance for them from the Trer of his Matie Navy.' To this concession she adds a further equitable offer: 'If Y^r Lo^pps thinke fitt, shee will give you security in the Admiralty Court for answering the said Masts to the right proprietor of them, when it shall appear to whom they rightfully belong.'

With this grand document (here cut to about one-fifth) the story, which has been so sharp and clear, tails off. The petition bears a series of endorsements: *The considering of this peticon is referred by ye Boarde* (Navy Board?) *to ye Lords and other Commissioners of ye Admiralty.* Ye Boarde sounds entirely willing to forego the pleasure of another personal encounter with Mary. A second endorsement plaintively enumerates the various court orders that she has successfully defied, and further than that the outcome is not revealed. One partisan of Mary has the firmest conviction that she kept the masts, or if not, that she certainly gave Council, the Navy Board and the Admiralty Court as much trouble as was humanly possible. But so often the petition has carried the broken begging voices of women without hope, or prospect of hope, that it is wonderful to hear an individual declaring her right, perfectly uncowed by officialdom in the shape of men or of documents. What a pity that in our generation the breed is increasingly rare—the breed of clarion-voiced Mary Thompson, unregimented; the Englishwoman Mary, magnificently unafraid.

III

TRADES AND PROFESSIONS
CONNECTED
WITH THE NAVY

THE King's ships were born in the King's shipyards at Bristol, Chatham, Deptford, Dover, Greenwich, Portsmouth and Woolwich. Each on its own river stood these gigantic workshops, a pandemonium of activity, in extent at least a half-mile square. Against the horizon stood upraised the ships in dry-dock, in all stages of construction; with the mechanical uproar of hammers thudding on wood or clanging on anvils, with the screech of sawing like pigs being slaughtered, were thickly interwoven the living uproar of men and draught animals straining at heavy tasks. Over the pungency of sweat rolled the thick black smoke of monster pitch and tar kettles forever on the boil, the raw smell of wood and the dusky smell of cordage being baked.

The servants of this seething cauldron of creation were mastershipwrights, master-carpenters, master-joiners, master-smiths, master-sailmakers, master-ropemakers and master-caulkers, all with crews of varying size under them. Servants of the completed ship were the master-gunfounders and powdermakers who impelled the beat of her fighting heart; beyond them again stood the victuallers, brewers, bakers and slopsellers who furnished her basic necessities of food, drink and clothing. On more outer circles of these chief professions moved a fringe of dealers in obscure and forgotten trades, and lurking beyond them a shadowy world of parasites, scroungers and thieves.

Hardly less interesting than a shipyard's men were a shipyard's commodities, being—up to the age of steam—timber, cordage and sails. Choosing a limited view, say 1620-75, we find little imported timber; it came chiefly from the King's forests, each tree separately chosen by experts and marked with the King's mark for felling. Private owners also sold timber to the Navy, but not on such a scale as later. Current papers seem to show little mention of defective timber, compared with the scandalous situation later. Kenrick Edisbury found, in 1637, 'very base, red and sappy timber' being used for shipyard repairs; also Jos. Tippetts of Portsmouth yard reported, 'Of the new forrest timber, much of it proves very badd; I presume 100 Loade of such may be pitkt [picked] out of ye parcell'. This is a high proportion, but the very rarity of such reports, during our period, makes them conspicuous. Of timber scarcity we hear as yet—likewise—almost no mention.

What we do hear from all shipyards, in accents of bitter and increasing unanimity, is the difficulty of land-carriage—of getting timber loaded into carts and hauled from the forests to the shipyards. This stumbling-block of haulage, above all, drove the men responsible for heavy ship-building programmes to extremes of desperation. Land-carriage depended, first, on local carriers, and local carriers depended on their own sweet will, being apparently so much in demand that they could refuse the Navy for what reasons they pleased. To this recalcitrance, the local J.P.s added their bit. No timber could be conveyed out of an area without a warrant from them, and sometimes the Justice was dilatory in granting it, or away from home, or provided other occasion of delay. But supposing the warrant promptly furnished, getting the carrier to honour it is another matter. 'I have receaved your warrant for 150 Carriages [carts],' Thomas Corbin writes to the Navy Office, 'Of which number I dare say not one will willingly undertake what you desire—conveyance of the largest Tymber.' A rising storm of shipyard protests over the decades is climaxed in February '63 by Daniel Furzer of Bristol yard: 'As formerly, the great obstruction is want of land-carriage.' He urges the Navy Office 'to minde [remind] the Justices what you doe expect,'[1] but such reminders if issued did little good, to judge by another of Daniel's letters with underlinings worthy of Queen Victoria herself. 'The carriers are much unsatisfied; I am forced *to steale time*

[1] SP29/68/43.

from other business in posting to and fro, first to the *Justices* for warrants, then to the *Constables* with those warrants, to warne the *Carriers* upon their delay.'[1]

These warnings are so generally ignored that at last—in March '64—a first-rate organizing mind is forced to bend itself to a prolonged and thorough study of the problem. Samuel Pepys, diving into it, comes up at once with one of those self-nullifying legalities that make headaches for everyone concerned: 'His Ma[ties] principall officers of his Navy Royall, although Justices of the Peace for their own Counties, cannot act therein as Justices of the Peace, but are forced to make their complaints to the respective magistrates of the Several Corporacons, wch occasions great delay.'[2] He goes on to suggest that if these Navy officials were made real J.P.s instead of merely titular ones, they would have authority not only to issue warrants expediting the carriage of timber, but could deal on the spot with shipboard disturbances in port, as well as 'fightings and querelles in and about his Ma[ties] yardes and stoores for his Navy Royall'. In practice few of Mr Pepys's suggestions were passed over, but whether the carriers gave a tinker's curse for this one would require a special pursuit of the subject over a century and a half.

Other difficulties in regard to the Navy's basic material float to us from here and there, disconnectedly. Launchings are dangerous things to put off, because the timber and the caulking may shrink; the enmity of time is helped by the enmity of the art worm, a dangerous borer; the widow West objects to 'letting her yard to lay the Kings timber in', and the King's Surveyor sides with her: 'I my selfe agree with the woman.'

More serious is the ancient and undefeatable question of theft disguised as perquisite—the workmen's perquisite of chips. 'The great quantity of wood carried away by the workmen when they go to breakfast, dinner and at night, is insufferable. Of purpose they spoyle good timber and cutt it into short ends, and hide these in the locked cabbins where they claime to keep their tooles.' Anything from a plank to a tree is claimed as a 'chip'; these thefts progress majestically in volume up to a whole shipload of stolen

[1] SP29/58/58.   [2] SP29/70.

trunnels (wooden nails) pounced on by Edisbury, to two men discovered building a ship with trees stolen from Dean Forest; still another man, building a ship, has taken 'beech 60 ft long for her keel, which tree was sealed with his Maties mark'. The Navy Office, supplicated to clear up this business of chips for once and all, replies despondently that the perquisite 'has been an ancient custom, and these men are a clamorous people hardly to be broken from their ancient liberties.' They offer some pathetic suggestion to prevent the stealing of timber: 'One penny a man per diem instead of chips', while the racket goes on merrily till 1806, when the formidable St Vincent stamped on it for once and all.

On two wild and wet spring mornings in '62 we may ride with two great ship-builders through storm-beaten forests on routine inspection, prior to felling. Daniel Furzer has found in Dean Forest 'of trees not lesse than 300, of oak and beech brooke'. Until this broken wood is marked as fit or unfit for use, Daniel thinks it best 'to forbeare [delay] the woodcutters, my experience having learned mee that they, through Ignorance and Wilfull-nesse', purposely damage a good deal of useful wood. Contrari-wise Phineas Pett of Chatham yard, kept from a similar inspection 'by Raine three days together, purposes to sett on Sawyers tomorrow morn, with all Speede'.[1] His reason: 'The wood will be much the worse if the sap rises.' But more bad luck holds up his programme: 'The gluts of Raine have not suffered the Sawyers to worke.' As for hauling the massive timber required for keels, 'the wayes are so deep that 16 horses could not draw it above 20 Rod without an overthrow'. Moving heavy loads from one place to another is a matter of terrible straining; to get a becalmed ship out of a narrow channel eight tow-boats are required, plus '60 yoke of oxen'. The shipyard itself is sometimes impassable, 'the wayes rotten with much rain, snow and ice, soe that the oxen cannot draw'.

Before the Maritime Museum at Greenwich an object seems to soar to incredible heights, yet this is only the sixty-five foot mast of a mere pleasure yacht, Queen Victoria's. Masts of a first-rate warship perhaps express in themselves the very altitude of timber

1 SP29/75/142

perfection, the tallest, straightest, finest trees; giant fingers pointing skyward, they and their cross-spars capable of bearing not only the drag of tons of canvas straining and whipping before gale winds or hanging leaden with rain, but also the shock of the pitching and yawing ship and the weight of men constantly climbing them. The creator of these towering objects, the master mast-maker, could afford to take a high stand, and did so. 'A Tender of Masts Maid by William Wood,' at £4-18-0 to £38 the mast, notes coldly in the margin that if the Navy Office want more, they must first buy up his stock in hand: 'hee will not contract for any to bee maid, till hee hath sold these'.

The masts themselves are as haughty as their makers, requiring special treatment; the tallest must be totally submerged till used. At Portsmouth yard they have been storing masts in the river 'from halfe flood to halfe Ebb',[1] but have now found 'a place more convenient and secure, a Pond. Smaller masts may heere lye afloat, and 100 of ye greatest masts may be alwayse kept under water. The chardge for ye sincking of 100 greate masts is £100'. Expensive, also the ponds must usually be rented, no simple matter. A Mrs Preston has promised her millpond to the Navy, but goes back on her word: 'She hath lately lett it for nine years.'[2] Well, murmurs the Navy, would this renter sublet it to them? 'She can give no positive answer until hee com,' and moreover pond rental goes up with each renewal. According to Peter Pett of Chatham yard, 'there are great advantages of Salte water to p'serve them; they may be kepte time out of minde, without the least damage,'[3] but salt water is not always available, and special mast-docks must be built to facilitate handling of objects of such tremendous length. 'An exceeding clap of thunder and lightning,' writes Captain Clark of the *St George*, 'ran down my mainmast to the middle deck'—awesome descent from aloft of a blinding visitant, and more awesome to be on the receiving end of it.

Cordage, 'the last hope of a ship, when her sails have burst under pressure of wind', evokes the picture of the fugitive flying

---

[1] SP29/80/46.   [2] SP29/98/27   [3] SP29/91/1

hunted before the storm, the wind screaming through gigantic canvas tatters flying uselessly overhead. The essential components of rope—hemp, pitch and tar—caused more problems than timber because they were imported, and also brought with them other unpredictable complexities. The manufacture of rope initiated by Charles I's Buckingham, under instruction of imported Dutch experts, is by now totally established as an English craft, every shipyard having its own ropeyard and hemp storehouse, and employing English workers only.

Sharp-eyed inspectors keep us well abreast of crooked trade practice in regard to hemp (also called yarn): 'Russian spun yarne appears faire on the outside of the winch, but is often false and ill-conditioned within.' Jos. Falkener of Woolwich ropeyard uncovers a variation of the same dirty trick: 'Rec'd from Sir Rich. ffoord 30 winches of Holland yarne; wee hanged up Nine of the sd Winches, and in winding of them off, wee found that they have put in ould white yarne spliced in short lengthes and covered it over with new Hempe; it is not fitt for his Maties service.' Other reasons why cables break 'from tendernesse of Hempe' originate in the storehouse itself, as explained scientifically by Robert Slater, master ropemaker: 'Upon a strict scrutiny, I find the cause to be the evaporation ascending from the adjacent piles of yarne newly Tarr'd; which condenscing into water and falling downe again on the yarne, caused that tendernesse.'[1] This excessive evaporation, in turn, exposes defective tar, 'which being of a more fluid and waterish nature, did send forth more vapour than usually; Insomuch that the topp of the pile was so exceeding wet, that I never saw the like before'.

Hemp in the storehouse overlong was another problem; Thomas White of Dover ropeyard reports, 'I have in Store 48 Reeles of french yarne from Mr Crucifix of Deepe [Dieppe]. I cannot get it maid out to roopes so soone as it douth require. And knowing it will be damnifyed [damaged] if it lye till winter, being full of Sand, I shall have it out into the Aire and Shake out the Sand and tarr it, and that will preserve it'.[2] To the peril of long storage is added the more dramatic one of spontaneous

[1] SP29/86/12.   [2] SP29/158/90.

combustion: 'Ye hemp lately received, being Wett, is very dangerous to be Laid in any Store house, for feare of fireing.'

With experience and skills more highly developed, came finely-drawn distinctions and preferences; Riga hemp was obviously the aristocrat of hemps. 'God send us enough of Riga; wee are cloyed with coarser sorts, always the dearer bargains.' As to the ship doomed by dishonest rope, we have a chilling contemporary witness both to the fraud, and to her fate: 'Old rotten and outworn stuff be smothered over with tar, that it cannot be discovered. By occasion whereof tall ships, rich merchandise and hundreds of the Kings subjects are cast away.'

Damaged or rotten hemp, actually, was an invaluable commodity; for wadding cannon it was called junk and for caulking ships, oakum. 'There is heere a store of hempe damadged, it will make very good ocum,' Falkener reports, but adds the familiar caution: 'The longer it lieth heere, it will grow worser.'[1] At times junk was sold: 'I did take notice of some refuse ends of Hemp intended for ye Dunghill, a piece of ill Husbandry; I caused ye Clerk to House it. And this day I am Offered 2s a hundred for it, and happ it may come to 4 or 5 pound.' During wars, however, there was never enough of it to sell. Cordage, in passing, appears prominently in the lists of stolen commodities, being easier to cut and carry off than wood or metal, especially if one owns a handy little boat: 'In the hould of one John Balloe his hoy, I have seen cordage to the vallew of ffour twines or thereabout, made of the Kinges stuff.'

The absolute indispensability of this article led, quite early, to proposals for domestic cultivation of hemp. In 1662 Parliament was petitioned: 'By Importing Forraigne Hemp, all encouragement is taken away for the planting of it in this Kingdom, and a manufactury of grand concernment is lost, the Poor of this Nation being unimployed.'[2] By 1665 Pepys takes up the idea so far as to write to a Mr D'Oyley of Shottsham, who replies that he is 'ill, very weake and farr unfitt to give you an answer'. All the same this charming and obliging man makes the effort: 'As to the proposition of encouraging hemp of English Grouth, in this

[1] SP29/51/38.   [2] SP29/53/52.

Country [county] wee hardly have a grouth sufficient to sett our owne good house wives on worke.'[1] Near by, however, 'there lives one S[r] Thomas Deerham, a very intelligent gent. and very steddy to the Kings interest, who can advise you.' A grotesque incident confirms the cultivation of English hemp: a dead dog has been thrown among growing hemp during the time of plague, and infected those who gathered the crop one month later.

Pitch and tar, after hemp the essentials of rope manufacture, were by one consent known as hard to come by, in all reigns. 'There is great need of tar,' Charles I is informed; may the writer buy three or four thousand hogsheads yearly from Russia, where it is cheaper than elsewhere? To scarcity, also, is added a problem we have met before. 'Wee doe finde our [new shipment of] tarr', comes a wail from Woolwich ropeyard, 'very unserviceable, by reason it doth incorporate into it soe much watter'—and this in spite of routine tests: 'Wee did at the first make the Usuall tryall as wee doe for all tarr, but it deceaved all our Judgments.' Our old friend Falkener also finds life complicated: 'The great Kitle [kettle] in the Tarr-house here is woarne very Thin and not fitt to be used any longer without great danger. I would intreate that you give Order to make a new Kitle, for wee must forbeare Tarring till then.'[2] Tar moreover has hidden dangers, as unpredictable as the infective hemp: 'Wee were ordered to put 15 last of tarr aboard ye hulke, but Capt. Badiley affirmes it cannot bee safely stored in her, there being a hazzard of Choaking ye pumps.' Other craftsmen give us glimpses of rope-making: 'I have placed the new STOVE near to ye furnace wherein wee heat our tarr in wch ye white [unprocessed] ropes are stoved, big enough to hold 4 tunnes.'[3] The workmen prefer the most modern equipment: 'The most votes are for an Iron stove, Not one for Charcoale. The first being thought safest, and certainest for working.' It takes five weeks for expert workers to make 30 tons of cordage.

In lost trade secrets, the mystery is not the composition of articles, which can be analysed easily enough; it is the *process* of manufacture that is lost, as for example of Coade stone, the only known substance that defies blast. Such mysteries would not

[1] SP29/140/42.   [2] SP29/68/44.   [3] SP29/151/43.

exist if all craftsmen had left as full descriptions of their methods as John Giles, maker of sailcloth. First he criticizes a rival's product: *It is soe Stiff and hard that it will frett and break in stress of weather, beside being so Boisterous* [unmanageable] *it cannot well be handled in a storme.*[1] Worse still, *it will mildew and Rott in a short time for want of due manufaction* [processing].

With John's sailcloth, on the other hand: *Wee Blanch and Scowre the threads and Boile it in a Salt Strong Lye for the space of Twelfe Howres, and doe use our utmost endeavours to make it soft. 1, that it may the better shutt* [be close-woven] *to hold the wind. 2, that the Sailers may the better handle it in all weathers. 3, that it may yield both wooff and warpp in stress of weather, when it is stretcht. 4, that it may the better preserve itselfe from Rotting in all Climatts.*

Between 1660–70 one of the top dealers in sailcloth was Mrs Constance Pley of Weymouth, who imported French canvas—considered the best—on an enormous scale. The Navy was chronically in her debt for sums between seven and thirteen thousand pounds, and always in such arrears as to reduce her to painful supplication. Also, from her letters and those of her partner, it is clear that—as with hemp—the domestic manufacture of canvas has been proposed, that the Pleys have invested in setting up the costly process, and are now in danger of losing their investment through the Navy's failure to meet its bills. 'If the weavers should be inforced to let fall their Loomes for want of munys it would be a very dificult thing to revive that manufacture again,'[2] George Pley warns, but it is Constance's heart that is nearly broken for inability to pay her workers: 'Pitty tis that I should meet soe great discouragement in soe good a worke, our English sayle cloth is highly Comended. For god sake sir,' she beseeches Pepys, 'get me an Order [to pay]: I only beg one word of incouragement.'[3]

'Sail canvas', the Navy Office reminds the Lords of Admiralty in January '35, 'is a commodity that cannot be had on a sudden,' and the drain is increased by 'the comon practise of captains, of keeping one shift of sails on board' to replace those damaged by weather, mishandling or combat. The skill required of sailmakers

[1] SP29/284/51   [2] SP29/157/46.   [3] SP29/137/87.

was high; Thomas Robins, petitioning for his late master's job, encloses a certificate signed by four master sailmakers that he is 'a fitt, able and trusty man' in his craft, also he offers something rarer, at least in the Papers: the certificate of Trinity House that he is 'the ablest of that profession'. In conclusion we have a bonus, 'a warrant for setting up 3 Masts at Greenwich, for drying of sails'—picture of great whitenesses outspread and upraised in sun and air, as if a ship had mysteriously foundered on land.

Inspection of sail-canvas, though later a part of dockyard corruption, in 1664 was very severe: 'I did view the Royalls Canvas sent in by Mr Harben; in 12 bails there is not much above one bail wch can welbe taken for a best sort.' Actually it seems remarkable that any unsatisfactory canvas got past, to judge by the official account of its reception into Chatham stores. First, it is measured; second, inspected by the Master Attendant to see if it is 'answerable to contract'; third, the Attendant makes out 'a Certificate of its quallittee'; fourth, he gives it to the purveyor, who may now apply for his money.

A constant peril of all raw materials—of which no aspect was easy—is that the men who inspected and used them had no accepted guide to their quality, no standard previously fixed; alone and unhelped but by their own experience and common-sense observation, they arrived at standards through their own improvised tests. For example, of the enormously important commodity of tallow (which depended completely on the slaughter of oxen) Ben Johnson of Portsmouth yard sings a variable tune: 'Wee have received two Casks of tallow, very Soft and indeed no better than grease; whereupon we tryed some other Casks, and this parcel is as bad as the former.' But now, interestingly, Ben takes it all back, having found out something new: that the usual test of tallow—probing the cask with an augur—is not a fair test of the contents: 'By breaking up one of the same Casks so pierced, we finde it not so soft or liquid indeed as we thought,'[1] and, therefore, concludes that 'the way of tryal hitherto used is not proper, it wilbe better proved when broken up,' announcing his discovery with excited underlinings.

[1] SP29/57/99.

The recumbent anchor at the Maritime Museum, raising its giant flukes in the air some feet taller than a tall man, reminds us of other specialists and skills. The chainsmith we have seen as well as his chain, each of its links weighing some three or four hundred pounds. Equally gigantic and ponderous was his fellow the anchorsmith's product, made by enormous physical strength wielding outsize hammers and pliers beside white-hot fires and huge water-tanks for cooling; also these Vulcans of epic chains and anchors needed, by many allusions, more assistants and larger shops than ordinary.

A letter from Coventry about a whole squadron with sails torn to rags after a fight, vividly illustrates the ship's dependence on her anchor in special circumstances: 'If the wind should blow in upon the shoare wee could scarce bear saile to gett off, soe must trust wholly to our anchors.' Unsound ones have unpredictable consequences: a final report on the *Anne Royal* states that she overturned in the river because of 'a defect in her anchor'.

But for all the desperate need of this succour in the ship's hour of distress, the largest-sized anchors are not easy to come by. The reasons, of course economic, are by no means limited to the usual one of non-payment. The overcrowded dockyard was a factor; John Himbrell, anchorsmith, is forced to petition: 'For want of accomodation in the yard where his forge is erected, to lodge his servants, they cannot worke early in the morning nor late at night, they being nowe not permitted to pass the guards as formerly.'[1] The stiffened surveillance was in wartime. Then again the anchor-smith cannot afford premises large enough to set up on the scale necessary to handle such monsters—not when the shank of a first-rate's anchor might be sixteen feet long. Henry Hall, anchorsmith, avoids this dilemma by specifying in his contract that he shall be 'allowed the use of the Kings shops'.[2] 'As touching anchors,' Daniell Adams writes coldly to the Navy Office, 'I ffinde that none of them have a Shoppe fitt for such greate worke.'[3] But this is not the only objection: 'Withall they say that they loose all their other Imployments of small Anchors, boults, nayles etc.' This refusal of large work recalls Daniel Furzer's

[1] SP29/72/42-I   [2] SP29/98/54.   [3] SP29/109/22.

sailmaker: 'Hee assures mee that hee cannot aford to make the Great sailes without the Small ones, which hee saith', mourns Daniel, 'doe make up his Losse on the other.'

Even with anchors wrung from unwilling smiths, the trouble is not yet over. 'Here are severall grt new Anchors', rises the irate voice of Thomas Harper of Deptford yard, 'wch cannot be weighed; a Stlyard [steelyard] is wanting here, for that service,' for until officially weighed, anchors cannot be issued. Ship-building also suffers when work on great anchors compels the smith to neglect items like nails and rivets, so that 'the Carpenters many times stand still, for want of Iron Worke'.

Obviously and urgently there should be a way of identifying each and every anchor in order to pin responsibility on the man who made a defective one. 'I have used my utmost indeavour to know who made the *Montagu*'s anchor', reports a frustrated storekeeper, 'but there is not any accompt of ye Smyths Markes kept. Care therein', he promises grimly, 'shall be taken for the future. Ye Anchors now in store are of Severall Markes, from Mr Hall in London and others.'[1] By this allusion an incomplete system of marks already exists, and it may be that in future every anchorsmith, like a silversmith, will have his registered mark.

'The *Mary Rose* is leaky, her box pump having sucked the oakum out of the seames under it ... A leake in ye *Happy Entrance*; it proves to be by reason of bad caulking, a seame left open.' Of all the nasty jobs in the shipyard, caulking was perhaps the nastiest. Endlessly in all weathers to move along the seams of a ship, stuffing them with the shredded rope called oakum; end-lessly to move along them again, pouring hot pitch on the stuffing; a dreary employment full of discomforts portrayed for us later. All this matter, constantly wet, produced horrible parasitic growths on the ship's side, while the goat's hair plastered on the bottom —organic matter contributing its own fungoid exuberances—did little good to the sheathing it was supposed to cushion; a state of affairs tersely diagnosed in Naval language by, 'Her bottom grows foul'. Goat's hair was delivered into shipyards by as much as four tons at a time.

[1] SP29/50/61.

Other workers in the wet were professional divers employed by shipyards to recover—or try to recover—what they could of sunken cargo or equipment, and a stroke of luck gives us the living voice of one such man: 'I did goe down [to the wreck of the *Charles*] but could by noe means find the Gunn that I formerly saw, although I brought up brass with an iron prong. I cannot goe down above twice in a week, by reason the winds and the Sea are soe turbulent in that place, and the water soe thick. I am afraid', he continues dramatically, 'that the hand of god or the power of Darknes is against me. Yesterday there came a Strong dreadfull ffish and swum round about, it had long gray Whiskers 5 or 6 inches long and some say long haire hanging downe, it lookt exceeding gashfully.'[1]

Cleaning a ship after long service was a strenuous job; accretions on her sides, hard as rock, were not to be budged even by the scrubbers made of 'brasse wyre', beloved of commanders. This immovable muck could only be dealt with by the process called *breaming*; big hot fires were built beside the ship, and the men called breamers literally burnt away 'weeds, barnacles, ould stuffe and other foulnesse wch the ship hath gathered under water'. The hazards of breaming were obvious: 'In the breaming the Shipp, she had very much Stuff upon her sides, part of which was melted downe. One of the men being carelesse in putting out of the fire, did Cause a sudden blaze. Wch by gods blessing was soon extinguished with noe more damage than the blacking of her side.' On a par with another breamer who 'was absent from the *Plymouth* when she was in the middle of breaming, and the fire on both sides of her', was the genius who brought in a lighted candle when cleaning 'ye Powder room of the Convective; it took hold of halfe a barrel of powder, and soe blew up pt of both ye Deckes and hath hurt some 12 men, 2 of them having Leges broke'.[2] There was no first-rate so proud that one fool could not make her a shambles of wreckage and ashes.

Luxury craftsmen, reserved for a *bonne bouche*, were carvers and gilders. A third kind, the lantern-maker (for some reason called platemaker or platerer) was the rarest species of all three, giving

[1] SP29/78/49.   [2] SP29/144.

himself the most airs; hard to get at best, imposing his own prices and conditions, and never to be obtained at short notice. Carvers were in good supply, the most eminent being the family of Christmases, and it seems that anyone called Garrard Christmas could be nothing but a Carver to the Navy by reason of his name alone, just as a man called Epiphanius Evesham must be predestined to sculpt effigies for tombs. Carvers' estimates give us an idea of these flamboyances in fullest splendour; here is one from Sam[ll] Price for a first-rate (abridged):

A ffigur of neption [Neptune] *Rideing on A Sea Horse Sitting on two Scollop Shells*
A trastle [trestle] *for ye head Cutt from Sea Anticks* [antiques] 2
  Supporters for ye Catte and rat faces Carved
A ffaire paire of kings Armes for ye Starne
An Ovall carved for the State Roome
A Belferie Over ye Cooke Roome [to hide a chimney?][1]

His total is £164, and he wants one-third in advance, one-third when half done, and balance on completion. For the King's yacht *Henrietta* the carver's initial estimate of £200 is lessened by the King's decision 'to hang ye Cabbons with Gilded Leather, and not to have much carved work',[2] which helps us see into the interior of these floating marvels; the *Henrietta* also had a white marble fireplace. Other estimates indicate the considerable pomp of even lesser fighting ships, *To cut ye Lyon with a scroule* [scroll], *To cut ye Kings armes with mantling and all proper thereto: with four maske heads.*[3] All this exterior carved work was heavily painted or gilded. By many allusions Charles I specified a great deal of gilding on the *Henrietta*, adoring brightness and display as he did, and this taste was shared by others; Tippetts of Portsmouth yard 'would gladly know what gold may be bestowed, besides that on ye Kinges Armes on ye Stirne; and', he hints delicately to Admiral Penn, 'I hope that *Neptune* shall not goe naked?'

That haughty and special artist, the platerer—always being chased with work—was the creator of those spectacular objects

[1] SP29/97/26.   [2] SP29/75/8.   [3] SP29/132/22

called 'a suit of lanthorns'—gleaming shapes airily upraised on brackets that, for all their strength, flowered up and over the lanterns into delicate lacy spires, coronals or crowns; shapes whose beauty seems better expressed by 'lanthorns' than the more brittle, modern, word. These affairs were anything but cheap; when the Earl of Sandwich wants three lanterns for the *Revenge*, Pett of Chatham yard writes darkly to Pepys, 'I hope hee may not begit you into the same charge by furnishing all the rest with the same number'[1]—evidently feeling that other admirals will follow the Earl's lead in this costly demand. Pett, while foaming at the mouth over a platerer's estimate, 'wch I thinke is very exorbitant', dares not turn it down outright. This constant difficulty of getting ships' lanterns is voiced by another Pett, Christopher, who is driven to appeal to the Navy Office: 'I intreate the 3 lanthornes ffor his Maties Yacht, ffor that I judge the King will expect to see them upp at hir lanching. They are the greatest ornament to hir, and are the most difficulte things to make that belonge to the platerer's trade.'[2] The ship models of the period show plainly enough why Pepys would have sold his soul to possess one of them. But the actual first-rate, advancing under full sail and full panoply on a bright day, with sunlight splintering off her brilliant lanterns and gilded carved-work, her long silk flags flying, must have been an overpowering spectacle; by moonlight, with her lanterns lit, a vision hard to believe.

Now that the dream and her humbler sisters stand completed, we have a list of 200 undreamlike objects needed to furnish them, many in an old language preserved only between covers of antiquarian dictionaries: 'Bilboes with 7 Shackles (a mutinous ship's?), leather Bucketts, Old rope for cackling Bittacles, hand lanthorns.'

Earthier still are the shipyard substances from which the dream was created: an inventory lists, 'oaken timber, beech, ash, deal and pine; ironwork, hemp, pitch, tar; duck, canvas; tallow, train oil, brimstone; copper, lead, goat's hair, horsehair; grapnels, oars, blocks, boathooks, anchors; broom bavins, sacking, reeds, calk, rozzen [rosin] and glew; ballast; flags, ensigns'. And finally, a

---

[1] SP29/99/138.   [2] SP29/79/115.

request from Portsmouth yard: 'If you will please to order 50 or
100 duz of lincks? They may be very usefull these long winter
nights, if occasion be of night worck; if ye warr proceed, it must
be Expected.'[1]

Farewell glimpse, over the centuries, of shipyards working
against time under the windblown light of pinewood links,
flaring dimly through fog and drizzle and the piercing cold from
the river, and through the long winter nights.

Victuallers, bakers and brewers present to our deep-freeze
mentalities, that take for granted every exotic in and out of season,
a whole vanished world of specialized knowledges and techniques.
The Naval supply of meat and beer was governed by iron laws,
and those laws were seasonal. 'This quarter [October] is the most
proper season of the yeare for procureing and saveing [salting]
the fflesh; for there will be very little Beefe to bee had after December, by reason of the want of hay.'[2] As soon as dependably cold
weather set in, the work was driven forward by the butcher-
contractors with a zeal commensurate with the thousands of tons
of beef and pork they must supply for the Navy. A very cold
spring for such work was risky, since it might suddenly turn
warm. Attempts to by-pass these natural barriers produced quick
and horrible consequences, of which one instance is a pattern
of all. In May, 1650, purveyors of meat received from Council
a rush order on the very largest scale; at once the butchers protested, 'If our lives lay at stake, it is impossible to procure such
supplies on so short notice, especially at this time of year, when
serviceable flesh is not to be had on any terms.' But the government, under threat of imminent war, insisted, and the repercus-
sions were instantaneous. 'Of 8 months beefe and porke in the
ship', reported Popham, 'there was not a fortnight's meat fitt to
eat.' The contractors, called to account, remind Council that they
warned of this very thing: 'We very much feared it, as it was
saved in so hot a season.'

The landscape of these mountains of putrefying meat is picked

---

[1] SP29/105/108.   [2] SP29/134.

out with individual exclamation-points of disgust. One admiral reports his beef 'so extremely tainted, that when the shifter stirs it, the scent over all the ship is like to breed a contagion'. 'At Woolwich', Vice-Admiral Goodson tells the Navy Office to its face, 'I finde the men are victualled with old rusty meat p'served with fiery salt; I have seen and tasted some of it myselfe.' Captain Badiley acknowledges an order to inspect beef, 'the wch I accordinglie have done. I find that for want of pickell and a good Soaking after, it is very mutch decayed, but to say that it Stinkes', he makes a delicate distinction, 'I cannot doe it'. To losses by natural deterioration, lesser calamities are added. '110 pieces of porke, steeping in a tub on decke, washed overboard.' At the very lowest depth is outright criminal practice: 'Dead hogs (not kill'd) cut up and salted and sent aboard ships. Measled hogs not fitt for men to eat, killed, cut and salted.' (Trichinosis?)

Beer on the other hand, unlike meat, depended on mild weather for its success, and a sudden drop in temperature might spoil a brewing of thousands of gallons. 'A snowfall in March has discouraged the brewers', a correspondent deplores tenderly. As a cause of shipboard mutiny, bad beer figures even more prominently than bad food. Nor is there any acceptable substitute: 'Their beverage is cider,' a captain feelingly represents the plight of his ship's company. 'They demand beer; cider is cold and unwholesome.'

By 1664 Naval brewing seems highly systematized. 'Stinking Beere taken on at Plymouth', reports a commander, 'was cast and throwne overboard.'[1] But he can identify it almost cask by cask: '25 Butt 1 punchin, 15 Butt marked with WH, 6 Butt 1 punchin marked with WI', enabling the Navy Office to come down on the brewers responsible. To replace the beer he has taken on '8 pipes of Beaverage wine', but has the most gloomy forebodings—and with good reason—about his men's reception of it.

Beer in fact is subject to more perils than solid foods. A brewer blamed for his defective product argues that his consignment was left too long on the pier, and in the sun, before being stowed aboard; it is this delay that has made his beer 'become hard and somewhat

[1] SP29/70/25-II

eager', Other caprices of this fairy foam, noted by those who handle it constantly, is that beer keeps better in iron-bound casks than in wooden-bound. An additional danger is noted: 'if a shipp's beer bee layd in 3 tiers, and the lowest tier in barrels not iron-bound', the bottom tier is sure to leak. In 1636 we find a chorus of pursers' petitions asking not to be held responsible for 134 tons of beer lost by leakage and 'by rummidging [pilfering] in the hold'.

Biscuit sounds harmless and uncomplicated compared to meat and drink, but it has its own dark corners. In 1637 one John Allen has bought 400 quarters of musty corn for next to nothing, 'not being fitt for the food of man', the charge reads, 'wch he converted into biscuit, and conveyed the same into the Kings shipps'. Bread from musty barley produced the disfiguring skin-lesions called St Anthony's Fire, and musty corn, if not having the same effect, can hardly be beneficial. About fifteen years later we hear Denis Gauden, a contractor, defending himself from allegations of bad biscuit: 'I have taken all the care I could,' he protests, 'it beinge my Ambition to deliver such Victuall as may be to the content of all.' But in a similar case another contractor, E. Wivert, offers a defense not only fascinating but strangely contemporary: 'To my great wonder I found a Complaint of ye bread [biscuit] in ye *Lyon*; when I victualled that ship, I took the exactest care I could.'[1] He then does the only sensible thing—goes straight to the baker, 'whoe told me it was as Good as any he had made. I tested it, soe much as I could come att, and did not finde the Least Signs of a mouldy Cake therein'. Then, unexpectedly, he digs up and throws at the Navy Office the real reason for the unsatisfactory biscuit: 'You may please to see in my letter of July Last [this is September] my dislike of a Sample of Wheat, and my reasons given of its Unfittness for your Service. Notwithstanding my great dislike thereof, I doe find that the Baker Used it on his own accpt [responsibility] and turned it into biscuit', so in the final event the baker is to blame, not the contractor. But tracing the bad biscuit all the way back to the sample of wheat is surely very modern?

[1] SP29/59/61-I

Curiously it is water, the purest element, whose chapter in Naval victualling is most corrupt of all. Water as a drink was regarded by seamen as a fate worse than death, yet water was a greater care of commanders than food, since the human machine tolerates lack of food for days, but lack of water for barely twelve hours without utmost distress. The wooden casks in which water was stored made it turn green and thick within days, yet efficient containers had to wait till the nineteenth century. The casks themselves created a problem of incessant demand and inadequate supply, a ship being supposed to return them at voyage's end by exact count; in 1666 we find Denis Gauden (now employed by the Victualling Office) noting the insufficient return of water-casks from ships. Coopers dying in time of plague affected the supply even more sharply; still another aspect of drinking-water aboard[1] perhaps offers, in this horror, a highest point of nightmare.

The greatest need for drinking water aboard, one might venture to guess, was for men at the guns during combat, when alcoholic drink, however mild, was out of the question. A team of five was required to serve every cannon; in an average ship of fifty guns, two hundred and fifty men would be used for this duty alone, plus replacements for killed and wounded or those horribly dead from the occasional exploding gun. The furious expenditure of energy without let-up, the searing heat generated, the deafening noise, the smell, the shock and jar of the gun's recoil, must have created a savage thirst for clean water, huge swigs of cool refreshing water, instead of what was available—the ropy stuff whose mere appearance made a man gag, and whose stench knocked the breath out of him.

And all the problems of every drop of beer and water, of every morsel of meat, came back to the single impediment of the times, the impossibility of long-term preservation of food; a ship victualled for a six-month period found her men at the end of it eating strips of salted leather that ate at their insides like vitriol, slimy beer and water, and self-propelling biscuit run on maggot-power. A concluding irony of victualling was that a ship to which supplies had to be rowed, might have the horn of plenty not five

---

[1] See Chapter IV.

feet from her side and still be unable to reach out and take it—
for a ship could not take on supplies of any kind if insufficiently
ballasted.

Over the turbulent kingdom of the shipyard presided a single
man, always distinguished by a title either by warrant or courtesy
—Commissioner, Commander or Captain. This unfortunate
person combined in himself—besides his basic qualification of
master-shipbuilder—the functions of labour officer, public
relations officer, union representative, impress officer, housing
officer and health officer; he also had power to impose fairly
severe punishments. He had to know every Naval supplier, and
the reliability of his product. He knew all about every commodity
in every storehouse of his yard down to the last tree-nail, and
probably knew most of the hundreds of clerks, artisans and workmen under him, both in their abilities and in their family circumstances. He fought eloquently for them when they were unpaid,
he represented other needs they might have, he jollied them into
remaining at their jobs when their bellies were empty and their
families starving and when the sentiment of the entire yard was
to walk out in a body. He had to deal with strikes embryo and
developed, with workmen's fist-fights and with quarrels of the
higher echelons like clerks and storekeepers, among whom
existed a complicated etiquette of precedence and a swarm of
professional jealousies. 'There is an encroachment made uppon
me,' one of them writes bitterly. 'Here comes Mr Harris the saile
maker and tells me he is sente to measure the Canvas. The
measuring of Canvas belongeth to *me*. And indeede that I should
have one putt over me, and the p'son a stranger to me'[1] etc.—one
example, from an anvil chorus that never, as a matter of principle,
had a good word to say for each other. A thousand petty rancours
the chief of the yard dealt with, by hook or by crook holding his
giant workshop together in the teeth of endless difficulties, by a
miraculous sleight-of-hand endlessly repeated.

Also the shipyard kingdom, restive with men, was restive with

[1] SP29/75/121

change—new designs, new methods, new inventions and improvements, for the art of shipbuilding was highly progressive. Yet in
the yard still lingered the grand medieval tradition of the heredi-
tary craftsman. Thomas Day, praying to be appointed master-
carpenter in a ship, is proud to cite his apprenticeship with his
father, Jonas Day, 'who in his time hath builded 180 shippes';
Richard Downey, nailsmith, 'hath from his childe hoode bin
trained to the making of nailes': Garrard Christmas, retiring as
Carver to the Navy, offers as replacements 'his sons John and
Matthias whom hee hath brought upp in the same art'. Men
obviously felt that handed-down skills, whatever they were,
added to their stature: John Jelfe, master-gunner, petitioning
for a job, notes that 'for manie years the Navie hath not
been without a Jelfe of special note and worth, in the arte of
gunnery'.

Our brief view of four heads of shipyards—alike only in their
staggering competence—might begin with Commissioner Phineas
Pett, head of Chatham yard, a born crook and a superb artisan.
Phineas first dawns, through the Papers, upon our sight in 1633
when his sister-in-law Elizabeth was suing him for £325 12s. 8d.
The large sum suggests that she had financed his apprenticeship,
and his gratitude took the form of slithering out of her every
attempt to collect it. At length the Admiralty, petitioned by
Elizabeth as a desperate last resort, orders him 'to show cause why
they should not give petitioner to take her course against him by
law'. Even this Phineas ignores for another four months, and in
January, 1634, Elizabeth has him arrested for debt as he is going
to church on Sunday.[1] A sanctimonious swindler then and for life,
he and his career were not affected by the gaol sentence. It was
this Phineas who was entrusted by Charles I with the building of
the first English man-of-war with three tier of ordnance. Here
follows an abridged copy of his requirements which he submitted
to the King, before beginning work; the localities refer to his
first expectation of having to build so big a ship in Newcastle
River, and the document gives an idea of the thousand things a
master-shipwright has to provide and foresee:

[1] SP16/259/10

That his Matie wilbe pleased to command
A warrant graunted unto me: for Materialls of all kinds
£2,000 for immediate expenses
£200 extra for the cost of getting supplies to Newcastle
3,000 loads of timber and other necessaries
Warrants for additional timber in case the first supply runs out
A warrant for a ship, the Black George, to transporte extra timber
A warrant for my owne transport to Newcastle in the little Pinnace
  called Henrietta of the guard of the River of Thames
Instrucciones from his Matie to the Lord Bishop of Durham, and all
  Justices of the Peace in that Country,[1]

to facilitate land-carriage of everything he may need. In conclusion he asks 'that I may receive no interruption, wch otherwise', he adds with the grimness of experience, 'I shall expecte'.

The execution of his royal patron had no least adverse effect on his importance, and by 1650 Phineas has risen to the dignity of Commissioner, chief of Chatham yard; his son Phineas junior is Clerk of the Cheque (paymaster) at Chatham; his relation Peter Pett is also Commissioner at Chatham, and *his* son Peter is master-shipwright at Chatham. Christopher Pett, George Pett and Joseph Pett and their families are all employed in some capacity at Chatham.

The predictable result began to give out a strong smell in the shape of delayed schedules, ships built of rotten wood, enormous embezzlements in the yards, and other closed-circle pastimes hallowed by tradition. The grossest abuses could be covered up with ease; all the Petts, faced with any threat of outside investigation, closed ranks and stood shoulder to shoulder, letting nothing out and letting no one in.

By November '51 suspicion was rampant in the Privy Council, the Admiralty and the Navy Office—'whisperings of grand abuses in the docks'—but obviously they had no idea how to strike at a clan so entrenched and above all so necessary. As a first attempt to find a weak link in the chain they fasten on a non-Pett, one Symons an ironworker, and try to get some

---

[1] SP16/287/46.

information out of him. But Symons, scared stiff, bleats 'that he durst not discover [spill the beans], for fear of being undone by the kindred'.

The kindred are the combined Petts.

'They are all so knit together,' whimpers Symons, 'that the devil himself could not finde them out.'

Yet, at this first faint whiff of probing to come, suddenly the whole yard is ablaze with every person or clique who has it in for another person or clique. One curious coalition is that of William Adderley, Minister to the Fleet and sworn enemy of all Petts, plus one Thompson, a caulker, and Thomas Colpitt a boatswain.

'We have observed much corruption,' they report piously to the Navy Office, 'and have spoken thereof to the Commissioner upon the place.'

This is Phineas.

'But he takes part with the offenders,' they relate dolorously, 'and is greatly enraged with us, and smothers up abuses. A genera-tion of brothers, cousins and kindred, packed together in a place of public trust, is not in the State's interest.'

The Petts are not the men to lie down under this broadside of righteousness, and Peter Pett briskly opens the offensive. He points out that Thompson and Colpitt are two of the most dishonest and inefficient workers in the yard, but his main fire is reserved for the clergyman. He scratches up forty-two signatures to a charge that the Reverend Adderley has neglected his duty of 'professing to us Christ' aboard ship on Sunday, so that 'the poore shipkeepers have been many weeks without hearing a sermon, whereby they remain without meanes of salvation'.

We have no precise statistics as to how the poor shipkeepers suffered under this neglect, but the same paucity of information does not apply to Minister Adderley. This clergyman, as virulent a specimen of dedicated hater as one might meet in a month of Puritan Sundays, loses no time in hitting back; by now the Pett-Adderley feud is so savage that Council appoint a committee to investigate. Six weeks later the produce of their labours comes boiling out in a series of charges and counter-charges in the workmen's own voices and their own laborious fists, a horde of grudges and enmities still crackling-hot and alive-oh!

John Brown, Clerk of Chatham ropeyard, is charged with 'having raysed divers Coyles of rope from the Docke for his own use. He hath borrowed from the Docke Twenty four boomes and Sparres which he should have restored againe' [and did not, obviously].

Brown answers the charges item by item, furiously but incoherently. Stealing the rope he denies in toto; 'he abhorres anie such cheate'.

But the choicest gem in this thieves' galaxy is easily the list of charges against Fred. Holborne, master mast-maker, '*and*', the accusers add pointedly, 'cousin to the Comisioners upon this place. The sayd Fred. is a Constant purloyner of the States Provisions, carrying away to his owne howse, divers parcels of sawne timber, tallow, bricks, tiles and haire [horsehair]. And hath had a bead [bed] made in the Mastyard with the States Provisions and at the States Charge, as allso Coffines to bury himselfe and his wife when they dye, which Coffines are now in his owne howse.'

Fred opens his answer with blanket denials, but 'confesseth that 14 yeares agoe he made 2 Coffins out of ye States materials and a bedstead about 6 or 7 years agoe as he thincks, and as he thincks he pd. for ye workmanship himselfe'. But the exoneration sounds uncertain and fragile, and Fred's signature is very weak and trembly indeed.

Now a tremendous blast is let off against the top man himself, Commissioner Phineas Pett. 'Hugh Frewin, sworne and examin'd, deposeth that he was present when 5 firkin Nayles and some deale boards were entered into ye Stores, but were taken for Com^r Pett, who hath not payd for ye same.' Robert Eason's statement tells how he has reported irregularities to Pett and Pett has told him to mind his own business and be careful what he says, adding as a reminder—and suddenly Eason's writing swells twice as big, like a suddenly-swelling voice—'THAT HE HAD POWER'. Other pot-shots at assorted Petts follow, through forty-eight closely-written pages of stiff crackling paper.

And the end of it all? It fizzled out damply, like most such upheavals. After all, what was the State to do with the four chief Petts? Imprison them for theft? Execute them for high treason? With whom would they replace England's most able and experienced ship-builders? So in the end the Commonwealth gives all the Petts extra money to induce them to stop stealing, for all that the charges against Christopher Pett and Phineas junior (the paymaster) are particularly serious and well-substantiated; their day of doom catches up later.

Doom, however, was still far away. For about the first six years of the Restoration the eminence of Phineas senior, if a bit tarnished, was still very considerable, and it might be assumed that this eminence functioned as protection for the whole tribe. Curiously enough the first underminings of the Pett totem-pole are traceable to the power-greed—equal to the money-greed—of Phineas himself. With the optimism of the cheat who assumes that others forget his past as easily as he does, he made himself conspicuous by his swollen-headed determination to establish his sole authority over Chatham shipyard. This involved him in a running fight with another employee over hiring and firing, and in subsequent clamourings for a warrant giving him topmanship over this rival—which he did not get.

Meanwhile, on the sidelines, other snipers are aiming at the Petts as a clan. By the well-developed Naval technique, in ships or out of them, of pulling a man down by indirect attack, they went—not for Phineas—but for his fellow-Commissioner at Chatham, Peter Pett senior. This target, no doubt carefully chosen for its vulnerability, caved in at once under the weight of over-ripe dishonesties and was impeached in December '67. It may be said at once that Peter, far from showing contrition or embarrassment, displayed on the contrary all the high indignation and moral rectitude of American politicians when caught with both hands in the till. But this first indication of a foundering dynasty emboldens a whole swarm of rats not only to leave it, but to attack the great Phineas himself. A deadly fusilade of testimony against him bursts out all at once, relating mainly to his cuts on timber purchase. The tough old man of course defends himself, upon which (July '68) we have a cold legal abstract of all relevant evidence in his case, which with equal coldness reveals his gross breach of trust and the hollowness of his excuses. Accordingly in September '68 his letters-patent of chief authority at Chatham yard are revoked. The general slaughter of Petts includes Christopher, caught running a private shipyard with State supplies, and more recently building a house for himself with prime shipyard timber. Christopher gets out of it by dying conveniently, the only Pett to escape in this manner.

Peter has now been impeached ('68-69) and conclusively booted out of his job; Phineas is now disgraced and suspended. Technically Chatham yard is Pettless; actually, we find both Phineas and Peter continuing to work there almost as if nothing had happened. The old, old story; they simply could not be spared. By 1670 Peter is caught embezzling from Chatham Chest —the charitable fund—and surprisingly it is Phineas who sneaks on him, indicating a serious rift of some kind in the once-indivisible clan. Yet to pin the theft on Peter will be difficult, a percipient man tells Pepys: 'You will have enough [work] to prove Mr Pett an unjust steward of the poore man's money.'

At this point the Navy Office, perhaps infuriated by Peter's artful dodging, takes it out on Phineas. They haul him up to London for an interview with a tough inquisitor, one John Cox, the same who had called Peter an unjust steward. 'I have had discourse with Mr Pett', Cox reports grimly, after a soul-searching interview, 'but am not satisfied with him', and announces his intention of inspecting Chatham yard himself. He does this within a week, and his preliminary report is so black that it lands Phineas before the Navy Board for a hearing. Oiled with plausibility and sanctimoniousness he slips through their fingers just as he did through Cox's. Now the Board, exasperated beyond endurance at his everlasting evasions, devise for Phineas a punishment which is—considering the man's gigantic vanity and power-itch—as excoriating as could be found: they put Cox in authority over him at Chatham yard.

From this vantage-point we now begin to have, from Cox, references to Phineas so searing in their contempt that they almost blister the paper. 'He is a great liar; I despair of seeing things

Title page *circa* 1660, showing navigational instruments then in use: compasses, azimuth compasses, astrolabes and cross-sticks for sun measurement, nocturnals for telling time by the stars, armillary spheres, dividers, rules and charts

A Ninety Eight Gun Ship on the Stocks.

Publish'd 2d Feb.y 1788 by Rob.t Sayer 53 Fleet Street London.

The Stern & Quarter of a Seventy four Gun Ship.

Ship on the stocks at Deptford, 1753, flying (l. to r.) the Red Ensign, Union Jack, Royal Standard, Admiral's Flag (the Fouled Anchor in an earlier form) and the Jack

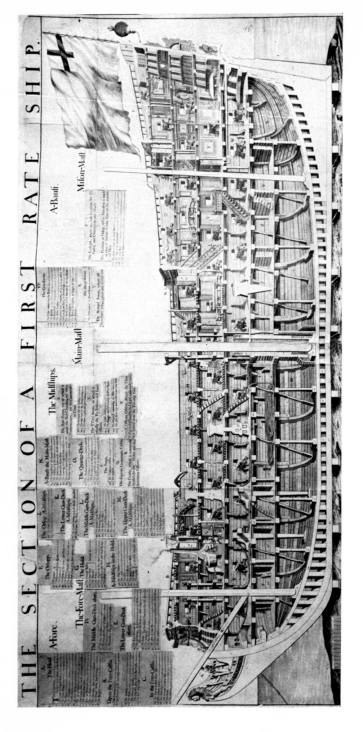

Cross Section, ship builder's blueprint, late 17th century

bettered while he is still master-shipwright. His workmen have got into slovenly habits and have no intention of changing them; the carpenters walk about with their hands in their pockets.' But even more damaging than such reports, the stony-hearted Cox has invented a programme of calculated belittlement, snubbing Phineas and countermanding his orders *in the presence of his workmen*. Naturally this produces, from the sheared mutton, a volley of anguished bleats for restoration of 'the power properly belonging to me [as] master-shipwright; it is frequent for Mr Cox to give me the lie before worke men, which must lessen my command over them'.

From now on it is war to the hilt. Phineas hires 60 men, Cox instantly fires them; Phineas 'brands' [queries] a bill, Cox orders him to take off the brand. This produces from both sides a terrific barrage of letters, one from Phineas running to sixteen pages.

Cox:　　The truth is, he is so much the gentleman that he is above that which he ought to do.

Phineas: He complains against me because I will not receive coarse rubbish timber purchased by him selfe, and have discharged his cousin, Brunsden the caulker.

Cox:　　I hope his malicious spirit, under pretence of serving his Ma^{ty}, may be discovered to you as well as to others.

Phineas: A rude multitude of women being wives and friends of worke men of the yard, it being chip day, I tooke severall carrying away a good plank; if countenanced, they would carry a ship out of the yard in their laps. [When Phineas tells them they can't, they retort that Commissioner Cox says they can.]

Cox now gets the Navy Office to query a timber bill of Pett's, and Phineas is well and truly in hot water. He explains his profit on the deal by claiming that the Duke of York 'was pleased to order I should be no loser by it, in consideration of my losse when I was suspended'. The Duke's qualifying of this alleged

permission (through the Navy Board), amounts to cold repudia-
tion, and colder still is the Board's reminder that 'you were found
trading in Naval stores', and their request for a *full* account of the
present transaction. 'The gentleman's stomach [pride] is come
down', jeers Cox, and certainly Phineas is singing very small
these days (January '72), and from now on refuses to touch a
timber contract with a ten-foot pole: 'I will send Mr Eason to
view Lord Winchelsea's timber; let *him* give you an account of it.'

In June, 1671, Cox has become Sir John Cox, Commissioner of
the Navy; a bitter pill for Pett. But consolation is on the way, for
on May 21, 1672, Sir John, being aboard the *Prince*, is killed at
Sole Bay. 'I have seen brother Cox interred', Phineas notes with
well-controlled grief; presumably he attended the funeral to
make sure that Cox, and not a substitute, was being buried.

And the end of Pett? The hoary old scoundrel's final dignity as
Sir Phineas, Commissioner of the Navy, proves—if proof were
needed—the dependable idiocy of the real-life ending.

So rapid and general a sketch must seem, from lack of space, to
exclude the Petts from all decency and humanity. This of course
is not so; every moment of their lives was not devoted to villainy.
Phineas wrote frequently to the Navy Office, trying to get better
wages for his workers: 'The storekeepers have a very great charge
[responsibility] upon them, and are allowed but 13d a daye; an
increase would be soe great an incouragement to them',[1] and
again we find him signing a petition on behalf of 'Mary Pullman,
relict of Rob. Pullman Master ropemaker deceased', and trying
to save her from 'the miserable assistance of the Parrish'. Above
all we are indebted to Christopher for using a singularly beautiful
phrase from the old lost language of the builder of wooden ships:
'The Caulkers were promised by me that I would indevor to
procure them a tide a day ffor the time they wrought under
water on the new Shipp.' This expression, *a tide a day*, refers to
men whose work on a ship depended on whether they could reach
it or not, according to the state of tidal rivers. When high tide
made the lower parts of a ship inaccessible they had of course to
wait for low tide, but at best it was a marshy job: 'By reason of

[1] SP29/106/72.

working in the wett and spoyling their Cloathes, the truth is they very well desarve itt', Christopher continues attractively. 'Ffor their labour in reeming the seames and placing of the Bilge waies is very hard, and they did follow it very closely.' This allowance of 'a tide a day' means paying the men for one high tide when they did no work. 'To grant the said alowance,' Christopher concludes, 'itt wilbe a greate incouragement to them.' An allowance to divers, of a tide a day, is also sometimes mentioned.

Brief outlines of Jonas Shish and Daniel Furzer, chiefs of Deptford yard and Bristol yard respectively, must be prefaced by a word on the shipyard strike. Many of these were caused by non-payment of wages; on such occasions there are countless instances of dockyard heads writing with painful eloquence on behalf of their men, or travelling to London to beg the Navy Office for some pittance, anything, to be going on with. For other reasons, however, strikes were so continuous that that admirable seaman James, Duke of York, actually conveyed by Captain Coventry—in November, 1664—his suggestion that a permanent labour-arbitrator should be appointed for each shipyard: 'His Royall Hignes aim is, that there should be a person of Ability and sufficient authority always residing there, [to settle] disputes, wch many times obstruct the Kings service.'[1] This is as modern as the sympathetic strike at Woolwich in 1661 when Christopher Pett, forced to discharge caulkers for whom there was no work, was faced with demonstrations not only from the men discharged, but from those still employed. Modern likewise is the Portsmouth rope-spinners' claim that 'to Spinne 77 lb waite [weight] of yarne is a Dayes work. This they finish about halfe an hour after dinner time' [knocking off between one and two]. 'Which time', laments the Clerk of the ropeyard, 'I cannot thinke a Sufficient days work. Rather than work Untill 4 of the clocke, they will not work at all'. Next day he reports that three spinners out of twenty-five turned up; the rest 'did goe to the alehouse'.[2]

It is Jonas who, in March, 1664, ran head-on into a sit-down

---

[1] SP29/104/148.   [2] SP29/78/105.

strike. 'By worent [warrant], all worke men att Deptford should worke from halfe an howre past five in the morning till halfe an hower past six of the evening. This morning they Came into the yard at halfe an hower past five. I spake to them to goe to their worke. they Answered not but there they stood still, till the Clocke strock six, and then every man went to his severall imployment.'[1]

This concerted and silent defiance—actually not a sit-down but a stand-up strike—infuriated Jonas into reminding them of their warrant, with negligible result: 'I receeve nothing from them but Evill Langewedge; for one worde I give them, they retorneth me four. They say hee, hee, what is hee, wee care not for the [obliterated, and perhaps just as well] of him.' The craftsman's pride of Jonas takes this hard: 'Sur, I Am Ashamed to see how Sloeley our work goeth forward,' and concludes despondingly: 'I will not trubulle yo no furder, but Leve it to yo Consideration.'

In happier moments he displays an unparalleled nose for stolen goods: in one man's shop 'wee found by Estimat 7 pounds and 12 pounds of Mixed Nayles wch are the Kings Nayles; and in the shope of Thomas Buckmaster we found puctock [puttock] plates and a peece of a Clampe wainge about 50 pounds wch he said he boute of 12 seamen wch were strangers to him'—old alibi—and Jonas has recovered likewise '2 peeces of hawser weghing Seaven hundeard pounds, and Ninety seaven yards of ould Saile cloth imbezled out of his Maties yard'.

The likeable Furzer at Bristol yard seems to have fewer labour upheavals than Shish; distance from London might have had something to do with it, or perhaps his own balanced temperament—whose thoughtful calm, while pervading the following letter, offers as well a picture of English shores forever encroached on by seas and silting-up: 'I humbly give my advice, that for the building a new ship, Lidney is not soe fitt a place as formerly, from the growing up of the Sands more and more against it; not knowne in man's memory before.'[2] It is Furzer again who lets us glimpse the expert's penetrating diagnosis beneath the surface: 'Uppon the survey of his Maties Shipp [illegible]: the risering [rising] of

[1] SP29/93/122.   [2] SP29/103/76.

her upper worckes bespeake Something amiss below; wch cannot be detected till the shipp be cleared and brought ashore'.[1]

This superb man, in the universal impoverishment of the war just over in '67, had to begin begging again: 'I humbly entreate money, that I may not be continually torne in pieces for want of it.' But such stringencies were common to all dockyard chiefs, and the integrity of his career seems as unquestioned as its success. Once and only once he was attacked: someone (it must have been from jealousy or spite) reports him as engaged in building small private boats. Calmly Daniel replies that he is not building private boats, he is instructing his assistants in 'the art of boat-building'. His answer is sufficient, or at any rate the question is never raised again.

These men of sober and honourable performance seem to stand midway between the picturesque sliminess of Phineas, and the brilliance of the rough diamond next contemplated.

Commander Thomas Mydleton (his spelling) of Portsmouth yard had spikes of character standing out all over him, like an elderly porcupine; not a word of his but reeks of individuality. By cruel perverseness of fate, however, his writing is such that the heart sinks as low at hundredth sight of it as at first; triumphantly indecipherable, it also reproduces in phonetics the peculiarities of his local accent. Anything blasted out of it, however, hews to the same jagged outline. He was rough, tough and crusty, with opinions like a descending axe. He loved ships and good craftsmanship, hard work, devotion to the King's service; he loved his yard and every sound and smell of it, waxing lyrical over 'a good sawdust fire and the sweet perfume of tarred ropes under it'. He hated laziness and slackness, he hated impartially any labourer- or seaman-shirker, he hated dishonesty with a special fierceness: 'Not the value of a handspike goeth out of my yarde without my hande [signature] thereto', he writes to Pepys, reasonably qualifying his strictness: 'We are but men.'[2] For thieves at night '6 good dogs are better than 60 men'; the dogs at least, he adds, don't connive at thefts. The perquisite system of the shipyard he despises, but has more sense than to advertise his

[1] SP29/66/67.   [2] SP29/165/69.

feeling—knowing his workmen as he does, and further en-
lightened by his share of strikes. With these he deals in his own
style; when some strikers retreated defensively into a ship under
repair, Mydleton 'caym aboard with an ax in one hande and a
playne in the other. To make all Smuth [smooth],' he cackles
sardonically. The Commander's sledgehammer vocabulary ranged
freely over a diversity of matters, including a Dutch prize ship
sent to his yard, which he considered unrepairable: 'Shee is an
old rotten heavy Flemish jade.' A pungent letter shares with
Pepys the pleasure of 'a ship with ye ould ballast therin. it was Soe
nuxsom [noxious] that it was A mistery that ye men on bourd
were not all poysoned with its stench'. His gift for reading character,
and an earlier professional collision, led him to despise Phineas,
after his fall writing disdainfully, 'I never knew Mr Pett so profuse
as to spend a sh on anything that was the Kinges', and adding an
extra jab about a creek that Phineas called '*his* creeke; I had thought
it was the Kinges'.

His favourite remedy for theft was the gallows—on paper. This
raises at once the question of the dockyard chief's power to
punish—never strictly defined in our source at least, but obviously
considerable. 'I having laightly taken a boye carying out in his
pokett some old Iron, I caused him to be sett in the Stockes, and
well whiped and the yeard quitt of him,'[1] Christopher Pett reports
to the Navy Office, with all the big crook's self-righteous condemnation of the little one. Mydleton, on the other hand, catches
a much more considerable thief red-handed and fulminates to
Pepys, 'The man must be hanged, beinge a very knave'. Yet he
backs down at once: 'Albeit I have profe, yet I know not how to
procecute any man to death, that hath stolen from my Selfe. If
I could,' he adds darkly, 'some had been hanged, that now liveth.'
His bark is of gallows but his bite seems to consist mostly of
setting pilferers in the stocks with the stolen articles ranged before
them, in full view of the yard.

The truth is that under his hard shell was a deep and unfailing
humanity. He appeals for his ropemakers: 'How impossabel for
them to supporte them selves without money or creditt, thayr

[1] SP29/96/108.

wages not allowed for 2 months, thayr bodies weakened for want of food.' His fellow-commissioner John Mennes is driven by the same situation to a turn of speech not unworthy of his colleague: 'I begg some money that wee may stopp the bawlings of these people, especially of thayr wives, whose toungs are as fowle as the Daughters of Billingsgate.'[1] When no money arrives, Mydleton passes on some bad news: 'All ye Ropemakers have discharged them Selves for want of money to buy food, and are gon into Cuntry to make hay.' Again it is Mydleton who reveals to us a petition quite unique, among a century of them in the Papers. Under provocation of gross and continual violence he has put some sawyers in gaol, but their release is out of his hands. What he does do for them is to forward to Pepys the petition of various women perfectly uninvolved with the prisoners, but who plead for them out of sheer neighbourly compassion and common acquaintance with distress:

Hen: Hunt hath 4 small Children
Thomas Craft hath 3 Children and his wife lyeth a Dying
Will Woodman hath 3 small Children and hath newly buried his wife
Henry Coleman his wife reddy to lye in
And if it please Yr Honours to looke upon us with a ffavorable Eye, and thinke upon ye Children and have pitty on them, wee poore women shalbe bound to pray for yr Hon^rs health and happyness.[2]

This document, the Commander confides to Pepys, makes him feel 'ancient and somewhat crazy'. Well it might.

Plague or other epidemics in the vicinity of a shipyard had to be fought with measures invented by its chief; there existed no national nor county agency to help him. Plague made horrible ravages at Gosport, where 'the graves are so shallow that they are commonly covered with crows and ravens, except when the grave-digger is at worke'.[3] Yet Portsmouth yard was affected very little—not by luck, but thanks to Mydleton's alertness and ingenuity. Not only does he move the stricken into a storeship fitted up to receive them (assuring Pepys that he has money

[1] SP29/126/100.   [2] SP29/152/26-26-I.   [3] SP29/161/61.

enough for this) but he turns another ship into a decontamination and quarantine centre, and institutes a strict inquiry as to the homes of his workmen.[1] The instant he learns that any of them have been 'in sicke houses, I ordered them on board ye *little francis* whair they wash them selves and thayre clothes, burning Rozeen [rosin] and Brimstone, and after 14 dayes I admit them to ye yard, and blessed be god they continue in health'. Not unexpected that the inborn reportorial vividness of Mydleton should preserve for us, out of the plague horror, an ultimate horror: 'Som of ye people in ye towne are soe wicked that they take thayre foull playsters from thayre sores and in the Night throw them into ye windowes of fresh [uninfected] houses.'

Yet in this tumultuous and brawling shipyard arena, one comes upon curious pools of tranquillity—pellucid and extraordinary natures, self-sustaining in their withdrawal. Inconspicuous beside Petts, Furzers and Mydletons, one such man was William Bodham, Clerk of Woolwich ropeyard. Of all unlikely products of such an environment, William discloses himself to Pepys as a sort of hermit-philosopher. 'For ye future I shall stick closer to my province, being delighted with its solitude.'[2] Of modest means though he must have been, he was willing to buy 'a Clock for ye yard, very necessary for many reasons: I will buy it at my owne Charge and keepe it without any Charge to ye King'.[3] The clock could live in 'a belfry or small turret', which he has found out would cost the yard only £30. Pepys' cold jotting on his letter flattened him: *Not thought necessary*. Undiscouraged, William rises to oratorical heights on the subject of hemp: 'Send us enough of Riga, and let all inferior kindes bee left to inferior persons, for baser uses.' His vein of highfalutin notwithstanding, there were no flies on William professionally; the great affliction of his life was short-weight—something he suspected of many shipments of hemp, but could do little about. But on a day of August '64 he is in the seventh heaven, having just received the very latest equipment, and can triumphantly demonstrate the exact extent of the swindle: 'With my new beame and sealed brass weights I tryed ye weights of the yard, and in every 1900 lib I finde there wants no

[1] SP29/150/75.   [2] SP29/V101.   [3] SP29/101/84.

lesse than $33\frac{1}{2}$ lib, by which these weights have Cheated his Ma[ty] of £500 in 4 yeares, and have given ye marchant 14 or 15 sh too much in every £80.'[1] Having made tests on every last weight in the yard, William sends the Navy Office an exquisitely-figured scale of 'weights too light by x pounds x ounces', and asks for 1,000 pounds of new ones. 'Had the old wanted but 3 or 4 ounces appee, I could mend them by driving some Nayles into their leaden Capps; but being soe far defective, tis past my power to cure them.'

Unassuming integrity lost in darkness of time and lost to us completely if not for the Papers, witnesses likewise—against the ancient charge of universal dockyard corruption—that there existed incorruptible men, dedicated to the honest building of ships.

[1] SP29/101/56-58.

IV

PASSENGERS AND CARGO

A ROYAL bride must surely appear, in all the endless throng of those 'passing beyond seas' in the King's ships, the most fascinating and romantic, offering in all aspects an attraction which few can withstand. The immemorial appeal of love, even if presupposed; the element of youth; the rarity of the event, only once or twice in a reign; the dazzlement of royal station, the vague atmosphere of carefree delicious wealth. In addition to all this was the management of such occasions, surpassingly skilful. The Navy, so harsh and utilitarian, for a fleeting moment became a fairy-tale flotilla brilliant with new gilding and new paint, dressed overall with new silk flags flying and the escort of attendant ships pointing up the uniqueness, the preciousness, of what the central ship carried—the star shining by reason of rank above all, the enchanted being forever unsoiled by everyday problems and miseries. This visitant from distant kingdoms also embodied in herself all beauty and all virtue, as did in their degree her setting of attendant lords and ladies—even if the actuality, on closer inspection, turned out a shattering disappointment. But such unkind realities are never thought of, in advance.

Royal romances, fulfilled or unfulfilled, carried with them strange complications and aftermaths. To find a royal young charmer for Charles, Prince of Wales (later Charles I), no effort had been spared; cheered on by his father who encouraged the project in a perfect dither of paternal love and romance, he took the unusual step of embarking for Spain to have a look at his proposed wife, the Infanta. This ill-starred voyage, long before it got in motion, evoked hollow premonitions: 'The *Prince Royal* is so much out of repaire that it will be a great expense to fitt her to goe to Spaine, and one way and another the marriage will coste as much as it will bringe in.' None of this deterred the doting parent, and the Prince sailed in early May, 1623; by July the King of Spain, prematurely optimistic about the marriage, has sent the King of England a gift of five camels, and worse. Than this marriage, of course, no failure has ever been more complete; in Spain the Infanta leaves off her high heels (chopines) in token of grief and disappointment, and in England James wants to get rid of certain appendages of his four-legged presents, in other words their Spanish keepers. The unfortunate Sir Francis Cottingham is first liberally soft-soaped, then landed with the baby. 'His Matie relyes upon that discrete handling wch you use in all things; inquire of those Spaniards who have charge of the Elephant and Camels, how long they intende to raine over those Beasts; his Matie [wishes to transfer] the care of these Creatures into the government of other people. By the graciousness of his Maties Disposition, hee will doe it by the gentle way of consent, if it bee possible. And His Matie prays, that the Camels may bee carried everie day into St James Park to bee fed, and brought in againe at night.'[1]

The next essay at finding a wife for Prince Charles was happier (or seemed happy at the time) and on April 24, 1624, an inner-circle correspondent sets out a brisk time-table of the romance. 'Tomorrow, an Ambassador expected out of France; the Contracte shalbe the 28, the publication the 30, the Espousalls [by proxy] the 1 of May. On the 5th the Lady beginneth her iourney; both the Queens [her mother and grandmother] do accompanie her to the sea side.'[2]

Actually the two elder Queens came only as far as Amiens, and Henrietta Marie never reached Boulogne till June 8; by next day a sailor named Thomas Ruddle arrived in Dover and retailed to its mayor some first-hand glimpses of the young personage, and the mayor, starry-eyed, passes them along to Lord Conway: 'Her Matie our gracious Queene came last night to Bullogne in good health (praysed be the Almighty) and very merry. Where he

[1] SP14/148/76.   [2] SP16/I/82.

saw her viewing the Sea, and so neare that it was bould to kisse her ffeete, so that her Matie was over shoes, and thence retourned with great pleasure.'[1] Breathlessly the mayor concludes that if any more precious bits come his way, Conway shall have them at once. In view of the later troubles of what became a love-marriage, and its tragic ending, one is doubly grateful to Thomas and the mayor for this carefree picture—the young girl on the seashore, the tide running up over her ankles, and her return to her attendants in peals of laughter.

The instant the bridal fleet gets to England we have some early notes of depressing reality, sounded by that incomparable letter-writer, John Chamberlain. 'The Q. hath brought they say such a poore pitifull sort of women that ther is not one worth the looking at, saving herself and the Duchesse de Chevreuse, who though she be faire yet paints fowly.'[2] Progressively gloomier, he points out that 'sixteene thousand pound of her dowrie is come along with the Q. wch will work no great effect, yf it be true that fiftie thousand pound of it is allotted for [various] service, and that she require thirty thousand to distribute among her servants'. By this ruthless arithmetic, £16,000 can hardly go far.

Six years later the gay young Queen herself not only supplies a passenger who is perfectly unique, but gives him a travelling-companion hardly to be imagined under the circumstances. She was importing a French midwife; to escort this lady to England she sent her pet dwarf, Jeffrey Hudson, eighteen inches high. On the morning of May 20, 1630, a port officer of Dover transmits bad news to the Warden of the Cinque Ports: 'At this very moment arryved a Barke of Callis [Calais]. The Master thereof doe most faythfully affirme that her Maties dwarffe with 4 women, one of them the Queenes myd wyffe, were all taken by pyrates. The dwarffe having at the leaste 2000 lib in jewells, and a waggone Load of Rich goods.'[3]

The King ransomed this lot of prisoners at once; the midwife, presumably shattered, went back to France, which forced the Queen to import another one. The advent of this lady was reported to the Secretary of the Admiralty by Richard Foggs, Commander of the *7th Lion's Whelp*: 'I received order to atend the coming of madam Peronne the Queens midwife. we had a very speedy passage wch shee seemed to be very joyfull of. praie,' he adds anxiously, 'will you please to acquaint the Lords of her safe arrival, as I understand there was grate care taken by them, that shee might be well accomodated.' Madam's joy was understandable; her next trip to England in December, 1635, had some unusual circumstances. The *Swallow*, sent to pick her up at Dieppe, was forced back twice by storms; the ship set out once more, with the captain hoping sourly that she would get there 'in time enough', and adding more sourly, 'I perceive they purpose to weare me out to the stumps'. But when the *Swallow* arrived at Dieppe they found that Mme Peronne had not sat waiting for them; she had bustled about and obtained other transport to England for herself and two nurses, and got to England on her own, brave resourceful woman.

Thirty-eight years later, when an English fleet is sent for another royal bride—Maria da Gloria of Portugal, wife of Charles II—we are lucky enough to have 'an Estimate of the Chardge of furnishing the ship appointed for the bringing over his Maties intended Consort':

A standing Bedd of crimson trimmed wth rich gold ffringes and lyned wth Satten	£1200
Thirty paire of fine holland sheetes and pillow beares	200
Traverses [dividing curtains] of crimson taffeta .	50
Trunkes, Chamber Potts, close stooles . . .	200[1]

With many other items the whole bill only comes to £1920, excellent value for so much gay harmless splendour—especially compared with Cromwell's nineteen million for an army to keep its foot on the neck of England. This royal passenger, whatever she was to endure in her married life—which Charles's cruel remark after their first meeting presaged ominously—on landing had at least a better Press than the far prettier Henrietta Maria.

[1] SP29/5/66.

'Shee is a very fine Lady', Edward Nicholas described her in June, 1662, 'and her Countenance promiseth abundance of goodnes. The Kinge is exceedingly pleased with her person and conversacon and certainly they are both very happy in each other.' Out of this too-roseate view, at least this 'promise of goodness' holds true of her journey through history—a transient unimportant journey, many times heartbroken.

Between the royal consort and the greatest peer there could be no comparison in point of glamour, yet a very considerable fuss preceded the coming on board of the Earl of Leicester, Ambassador to Denmark (April, 1632): 'His Lordship will have at his owne table, besides him selfe, some 8 or 9, some 10 gentlemen attendants, and some 20 besides of serving-men, footmen and cooks. Take care to send into his ship, a buck or two baked in pies, and 4 or 5 of the fairest chines of beefe, pickled and some wine.' In May '58 Cromwell himself issues some strict orders, not on the score of luxury but of behaviour: the wife of a diplomat is travelling 'with her servants, to the Hague; take especial care that she is treated with due respect answerable [suitable] to her degree and quality'. For all the legend of Puritan austerity, their ambassadors to Holland took with them magnificent services of table silver. In fact the elaborate provision for higher servants of the State, bound on official business in the sixteenth and seventeenth centuries, is not the least fascinating aspect of travel in the King's ships. The common miseries of a small rolling and pitching vessel were of course inescapable, but were palliated—even if unavailingly—by every amenity procurable.

For all that H.M. ships were non-passenger ships, the volume of voyagers in them is bewildering in its incessant and restless diversity. Royals and nobles and their suites, State servants great and small, persons of anonymous identity such as spies, convicted felons and scrapings of the gutter forcibly rounded-up and sent abroad for colonization—all this gigantic unrolling tapestry and seaborne pageant was woven in every colour of fortune or adversity, from gold-and-crimson pomp to grey verminous misery. Out of the surging procession there looks an occasional name from the empyrean, alien in the context of civil servant (May, 1658): 'Mr

Milton to submit a list of such persons of his retinue as he wishes to carry with him, that the same may be affix'd to his pass.' He took seven clerks with him to the Holland Peace Conference.

Quite different, as to care and comfort, were Commonwealth's proceedings in the case of another royal passenger: 'Order from Parliament; to move Henry Stuart, third son of the late King, and the Lady Elizabeth, to a fit place beyond seas.' The ponderousness and callousness of the machinery set up to deal with one little boy of eight or so, and one sickly little girl near her death, must be followed through the Papers to be believed; of the committee appointed, sufficient to note that it sat for two years and seven months (1650-52), adding or dropping members as it went along. Over this interval Elizabeth of course has died, and the deterioration of Henry's health at damp cold Carisbrooke is regularly reported by his guardian-gaoler, Mildmay, and as regularly ignored by the committee. Meanwhile they argue endlessly 'the disposing of Henry Stuart'; first to Heidelberg, then to somewhere else, then at last 'to any port in Flanders'. The tiny vessel he finally boarded at Cowes on February 13, 1652, was hired by the State, therefore technically it was a Commonwealth ship. For all the secrecy observed in getting him aboard for fear of public demonstration, some privateers in the road shot off a salute to the Duke of Gloucester. Storms promptly drove the ship into Dover road and detained it there for three days.

After this William Cullen, mayor of Dover, takes up the tale; the ship's master, obviously alarmed lest his passenger die on his hands, has been driven to share the responsibility with someone else. 'The said Henry Stuart being incommoded through 3 nights distemper at sea,' Cullen reports to Council, 'I have put him into a private house at Deal, and humbly hope it will be in no way displeasing to the State.' Carefully he adds that the little boy has been smuggled there with every precaution against publicity, begging pardon for his offence in taking a wretchedly seasick child out of the cockleshell where he has been tossed about for three days and nights. It had taken the government two and a half years to dispose of Henry; it took them exactly twenty-four hours to shoot back a grim letter to the port officer at Cowes, asking for the names of the ships that saluted Henry.

Out of the lesser mass or official comings and goings occasionally blooms a bright flower of allusion of compliment. When Dudley Carleton's wife insists on accompanying him abroad during the worst of the pirate menace (1609) a friend writes him that 'shee deserves thanks for her love, and prayse for her valour'. On lower levels, also rarely, flashes a bizarre streak in colours of murder. Edward Woodshaw, paid government spy habitually crossing in the Queen's ships, in 1574 writes to his employer, Burghley, 'I will at your Orders go to Spaine, and wisely and faithfully gather intelligence; or if you will sende me a lingering poyson, I will have it given to anie you please.'

From this obliging and beautiful nature we fall headfirst into the stench and darkness of the holds (October, 1618) in which 'the Citie is shipping to Virginia a hundred younge boyes and girls that lay starving in the streetes; wch is one of the best deeds that could be don with so little charge, not rising to above 500 lib'[1]—wild filthy young animals, alive this far either through cunning, or mere ferocious will to survive. The girls in these ships, in common with women transported in the hulks up to and past 1800, figured as willing partners in the unchecked promiscuity attested in the several pamphlets produced by half-literate seamen.

Yet below the poverty-cursed and disinherited, a proclamation of August, 1622, indicates a darkness still lower: 'Persons attainted of felony (except murder, rape, witchcraft, highway robbery, arson or burglary) are to be transported beyond seas and putt to hard labour usefull to the Comonwealth, untill by certificat of good conduct they are remitted.' Whether criminal by nature or by destitution, without distinction voyaging in manacles stapled to walls, living below-decks on fetid air and vile provender, some of this element—nevertheless—might be at large in the ship: 'Warrant to reprieve such convicted felons as, for strength of bodie, shalbe thought fitt to be employed on voyages of service beyond seas.'

[1] SP14/103/33.

Phineas Pett, Master Shipwright, and
Sovereign of the Seas, 1637

Stern of *Sovereign of the Seas*, 1637. Designed by Van Dyck, executed by John and Matthias, sons of the famous Garrard, all three 'Master Carvers to the Majesties Navie'. The three tier of ordnance, Charles I's conception, are clearly seen

Queen Mary's Barge or Shallop, *circa* 1690. Royal Arms
and other ornamentation possibly by Sebastian Vicars,
Carver to the Navy

Portable globe in leather case, early 18th century

Mudge Chronometer. Inscribed: 'Invented by Thoˢ Mudge for the Benefit of NAVIGATION and rewarded by the BRITISH PARLIAMENT Anno Domini 1793'

Side view of the Mudge Chronometer

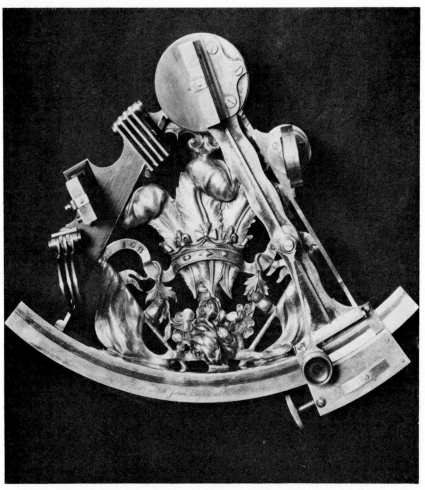

Sextant made for Albert Edward, Prince of Wales, 1853.
Silver and gold. A late example of the ancient tradition by
which utilitarian objects for royal use must be made of
precious metals and with the most elaborate workmanship

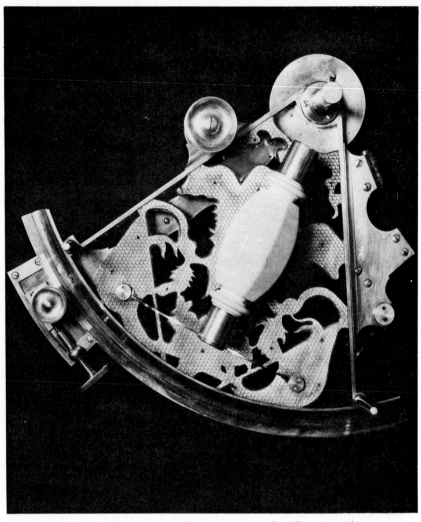

Back of the sextant, showing ivory handle. Signed, *Mrs. Janet Taylor, 104 Minories, London.* She was a leading ship's chandler and instrument maker

With this possibility there seems completed, if not the full circle of passengers, at least the full circle of a social order, from the royal bride in her floating gilded palace to another sort of bride: the one chosen out of the hulks for a colonist's wife, and perhaps already pregnant by some anonymous seaman, or seaman-criminal, of the voyage.

Cargo in the commercial sense was of course no affair of the King's ships, yet many odd things found their way into them for various reasons, and innumerable small objects were confided to captains for families or friends. Thanks to an item of June, 1662, we not only glimpse some intimate domestic arrangements for a royal bride, but also the method of shipping them, since packing is in itself an interesting art.

A list of things for the service of the Serenissima Queene: wch not being usefull here: are sent backe into Portugall by her Royall Maties Order:
Twelfe Trunkes covered with Leather wth Gilted Nayles, ffourteen Box chests in wch were sent Beds, One cloathe chayre wth Gilted Nayles, Two large greene Velvett Sackes wth Severall Quiltes.[1]

A constant cargo-item in Naval ships, surprising in its mass, was the traffic in animals. Kings, princes and nobles were forever sending each other expensive presents of horses, hounds and deer to stock royal preserves. These valuable creatures had to be taken great care of, and great care was taken; nevertheless circumstances beyond control often drove their custodians crazy. One such man, John Lanyon, lifts his voice from Plymouth in August, 1662. He is charged with the fearsome responsibility of 94 horses, and in his situation there is nothing agreeable at all: 'The 94 horse are aboard 2 ships, but the Convoy appeares not yett.' Meanwhile, for the poor animals penned up in semi-darkness, 'I shalbe forced to re-execute [re-order] their p'vision of oats and hay.' But beyond oats and hay looms something truly frightening; 'The

[1] SP29/55/40.

caskes wch have layd empty since the last voyage, will not hold water.' Imagine the horrifying moment when a man, going confidently to unused casks during a long voyage, finds their contents all leaked away. For Lanyon it must have been desperate; he could not offer promises or explanations to ninety-four horses.

In 1661 Charles sent a ship to Germany 'for the fetching over 120 Stagges from Hambrough, sent to the Kinge by the Elector of Brandenburg'. Nor was Charles behindhand in returning the courtesy: 'Passe to transport 12 couple of hounds and a mastiff to the Elector.' Parrots sometimes came to England with envoys returning from exotic lands, and in April '62 a couple of pelicans went to France under the chaperonage of Sir William Ravy. The suffering involved, in the small ships of the period, must have been indescribable for horses especially; flung about in their stalls during storms, hurt and terrified with the four-legged terror beyond assuagement. One consoling note is that every care was used to send them during the more clement months of July and August, though one captain has bitter things to say about horses shipped in winter.

When commercial merchandise in quantity appeared in a King's ship, it came invariably from a single source: prize cargo ships too badly damaged to tow in, and hastily unladed as far as possible into the captor ship. One such prize was leaking and her cargo was sugar; with understandable speed '662 Chests of Sugers' were transferred. Commanders of Naval ships were by no means regarded as above suspicion, where tempting items of cargo were concerned. In one case an angry and self-justifying commander, Captain Thomas Bardsey, assails the Navy Office without preamble: 'Concerning the Chest of Camphire wch I am taxed withall; it will appeare by this noate in whatt kind [manner] I did.' He explains that he *has* borrowed a quantity of camphor from this chest, on the prospect of being short of money; the prospect not materializing, he put it back again. 'As for the 6 elephants teeth', he continues with bitter sarcasm, 'this after-noate will show what money I had for them, soe that noe man shall prove me other than honest.' The 'after-noate' (attached memorandum) is a receipt for 6 elephants' tusks, surrendered to the Customs at Cork. That the presence of these objects in his ship remains unexplained forever-more, merely adds to the pleasant fog surrounding the subject.

It may be remembered that in 1625 Charles I, trying to prop up his ravaged kingdom, pawned a huge quantity of plate and jewels in Holland. Now in 1637 he is able to redeem some of them. By largesse of the contemporary English that could make a routine bill of lading read like poetry, this flashing inventory is not less poetic:

1, *A pommel of a Sword garnisht with Dyamonds*
2, *Cuff cauled the Constables Cuff garnisht wth Rubies and Dyamonds, weighing fffty Eight ounces*
3, *jewell cauled the three brethren, in the fforme of a fflower wth three great rubies ballais, three great pearles, and one pendant pearle*[1]

After these is listed, by exact number, masses of pearls in ropes and 'loose pearles for buttons', which illustrate the professional method of sending them: large sheets of cardboard were coated with jeweller's special 'hard waxe' and the pearls gently pressed into it while warm, then the whole thing was crossed and recrossed with ribbon. The full weight of pearls, cardboard, wax and ribbon was meticulously noted, and the inventory endorsed: *A true list of his Maties jewells redeemed out of Holland by Job Harbie. Signed and attested by Sr William Boswell, English Resident at haghe* [the Hague].

But of all this treasure-chest of the Papers, prodigally over-flowing, the real jewels are not the King's diamonds nor prize-ship plunder however rich, but the occasional charms or amulets that one friend concerned for the health of another would send in care of an obliging Naval captain. Fragments minute, unclassifiable, nevertheless they are points of light upon a whole world of vanished beliefs and superstitions long remote from us. In 1582 a friend of Walsingham's writes, 'I send you 3 little cushions of arsenic, to bee hunge around the necke, and reste upon the harte, as preservations against the plague'. But even the arsenic cannot compete with William Willett's offering, in April, 1630, to Edward

[1] SP29/369/46.

Nicholas: 'I send in a box, a Mermaides hand, with a ribb. Wch is said to be good to Make Ringes for the Crampes, and to stop bludd'—an item leaving behind it the problem as to whether a piece of mermaid should be considered cargo, or called a passenger.

V

INVENTIONS AND DISCOVERIES

THE technical aptitudes of man have been astounding in all ages, appearing to surmount the limitations of the knowledge, facilities and materials that bound them. Not least among these powerful executants were the shipbuilders who—in the sixteenth and seventeenth centuries—brought the handling of wood to the highest perfection it has ever achieved.

With England living for centuries under the shadow of attack, threatened or actual, the emphasis of invention lay naturally on means of defence and navigation. The constant flow of inventions through the Papers reflect the individual awareness of this shadow, and lead us to the man at his solitary toil in cellar or shed, striving to give form and substance to the fragile thing in his brain, the idea as yet unborn.

This lonely and absorbed figure had, in his day, no more help than inventors before or long after him; unaided he fought his way through endless experiments, through endless labour of bringing it to a point of dependable performance, and through other rigours of constructing what he must offer to prove his claims, a working-model as nearly perfect as possible. Having achieved this, no way lay open to him but the one of petitioning some highly-placed person and of getting him to see it in action. If the demonstration were successful he could then petition the King for exclusive rights of manufacture and profit, which were usually accorded for a term of fourteen years in consideration of a nominal fee to the Crown, perhaps five pounds a year.

The present chronicle of invention brings to light two post-scripts, one good and one bad. The good one is that the traditional view of the inventor as born to neglect and obstruction must, in the case of ordnance, be modified; any man who produced an improved method of killing could without fail get important people to look at it, and such people seem—by record— remarkably able to sort out useful ideas from the claims of visionaries or cranks. The bad one is that the story of these discoveries is almost never completed in the Papers; perhaps most such endings lie buried in the records of Ordnance. Of one story given entire by our source, the ending is unhappy.

With the accession of Charles I, a King in love with ships and eager to give special attention to everything connected with them, it is interesting to see the tremendous response evoked. No use submitting ideas to the ill, uninterested old King, the father; all this pent-up thought burst out and flowed in a mighty surge toward the new King, the son. In December, 1625, a letter from William Betts, 'Master Gunner of his Maties shippe the *Victorie*' claims that 'I have found a meanes to cast a gunn shall shoote an iron bullet from one pound weight to 5 or 6, much further than a muskett; and may be made soe light that a Man may carry one of them. Alsoe I have invented a fier ball that may be shott out of any ordnance from a Saker to a cannon; of these balls noe man ever made or had the use of, but my selfe.' He ends unexpectedly with an appeal, that cry from the soul of all inventors, lest 'these works, and many others which lye dead in mee, may die as well: I having no meanes to bring them to light'.[1]

One month later William Engelbert comes up with a plan to destroy every harbour in Spain, 'as that never Shippe of Burthen shalbe able to goe in or out of them more'.[2] He is ready with 'a modell of the Ingen, that shall performe the aforesaid,' and offers it for demonstration. Almost simultaneously Henry Norwood has found a way to intensify the effect of liquid fire (already well-known), engaging 'to make Waters to fier ships, or any other combustibel matter'.[3] He has also been studying propulsion, offering 'to cause any cannon to carry hir bullett as farre again as ordinary, with the same powder and charge,' and likewise a

[1] SP16/12/96.   [2] SP16/21/110.   [3] SP16/22/23.

method 'to trimm any Wood in that manner, that noe fier shall burne it; good for shippes in a Sea fight'.

This dream of fire-proofing ships was patently shared by Charles I; a document of two enormous pages, crowded with elaborate provisions and sub-provisions, shows how seriously he took it. 'Whereas William Beale hath by his own Study and Industrie brought to p'fection a new invention by him found out, how by the applyance of compounded Stuffe and Water called Cement, shippes may be preserved from burning by fire or Gunpowder in fight at Sea . . . .'.[1] Marvellous as this is, the cement can do something equally good in the view of a King dedicated to the commerce of his nation: ships painted all over with this cement before going on long voyages might 'without Sheathing be preserved from hurt by the Sea worme or barnacle, whereby manie shipps of great value are oftentimes utterly Spoyled'. [Therefore, wishing] 'to encourage all such ingenious inventions as tend to the Publique Safetie', he gives Beale exclusive rights to manufacture and profit for 14 years, but adds some unusual restrictive clauses 'that hee, his heires and assignes' may on no account offer the formula to any foreign power whatever, on pain of severe penalty.

A few weeks later we have the rare experience of attending the test of this fire-proofing solution, when in July, 1626, Joseph Reynolds, an Artillery officer, reported to the Navy Office: 'Whereas I was required to receave into the Artillerie Gardens a certaine frame of treene oaken planke about fower foot square, breamde with the Stuffe or Myxture wch one Wm Beale pretended [claimed] no fier should burne: I sett the frame upright like a shippe side, and putt thereto a fier Ball made some 14 years since: and it melted off most parte of the Stuffe, and burnte into the planke. Wch Stuffe falling downe to the grownde fiered and flamed most forciblie,'[2] so that if the test had been made in a shipyard, Reynolds concludes, it might well have touched off a raging conflagration. His satisfaction in the failure is evident; rumour of the invention must have caused much professional jealousy, to say nothing of the inventor's highroad to the King's favour. The disappointment of Charles, on the other hand, must

[1] SP39/18/55.   [2] SP16/31/37.

have equalled his high hope of what turned out simply too good to be true; a sound idea, as yet beyond man's technical grasp.

The horror of fire at sea engaged men's minds continually, and not seamen's minds alone by any means. In 1631 'Thos Grant, Doctor in Physic,' gets exclusive rights in his invention called 'a Water Bow, for preservation of Ships on fire'; also there survives a memorandum, no more, of a warrant: *Invencon to quench fire in Shipps of Warr; to raise Water; Hen. Robinson is granted whole use of etc.*[1] They sound respectively like a high-pressure hose and an emergency high-speed pump, and the grant of exclusive rights implies—as will be seen—that both contrivances have been tested successfully.

In conceptions of attack and defence, revolutionary is the only word for those of 'Erasmus Purling, ingenieur', in 1665: 'a Warlike Ingine with 100 oares, all in Covert, in Security from any Shott; with this said Ingine I shall undertake for to enter into the middle of any fleete and destroy them, without danger from [weapons] or men'[2]—in other words a ship designed without the vulnerable open decks, totally enclosed but for gun-ports, perhaps metal-sheathed; a Carolean prototype of the *Monitor*, 'the armored cheese-box' of the American Civil War. Equally revolutionary are the ideas of Captain Samuel Carington, for under-water and above-water explosives operating on the principle of the time-fuse, with a delayed-performance range of up to two days; he also claims to have 'studdyed power never yett putt in Execution by any man living; ffyreworks that without fayle Execute [discharge] att Sea or land or under ye Water, of their owne proper motion, from halfe an hour to forty Eight hours distance of time'.[3] But no more is disclosed, by the Papers, of this frightening prophet of the future.

Native inventors like the above at least had the advantage of displaying their wares on their own home ground; foreign inventors living in England might find their position less favourable. In such a case Martin Beckman, Swedish captain of artillery, took the sensible step of approaching distinguished foreigners in England, as stepping-stones to English circles of influence.[4] His

[1] SP29/113/141-I.   [2] SP29/150/23.   [3] SP29/106/86.   [4] SP29/206/176

methods are more interesting than his invention (another incendiary missile), for he has demonstrated his idea successfully enough to address the King direct: 'Uppon Tuesday last I did try it in ye presence of Count Konigsmarck and many other officers; and intend this week to doe it again in ye presence of other witnesses. I can doe great Service against your enemys the Dutch,' he claims, and also reveals a bitter personal feeling: 'I would willingly venter my life and blood to reduce them into misery, for the wronge they have done me.'

Inventions more pedestrian survive in numerous petitions after the inventor's death, for renewal of exclusive rights in patent swivels and other properties: 'Dorothy White, Part Owner of Chaines laid in the River of Thames; her deceased husband having invented a Meanes of Moaring Shipps with Chaines, to ye great preservation of Shipps and Cordage, and granted the sole benefit thereof for ffourteen years'.[1] The time being about to run out, she prays for an extension.

After lethal weapons and swivels and chains we come to the true delight—the calm port of voyaging minds which belonged neither to seamen nor fighters but to men who, in some quiet study or garden, laboured for greater precision of theory or of instruments useful to ships, for purposes other than war. The following petition dispels, by allusion, the grotesquely-false impression that the second Charles was an impulsive light-weight compared to the first. It has been seen how eagerly Charles I leaped at Beale's fire-proofing process; by the following document we may see with what caution and reserve his son would have treated a similar claim. 'Petition of Hugh Chamberlain MD, who desires a Patent for ye invencon of making Ships to saile within 2 pointes by helpe of the Wind.'[2] Courteously the King replies, 'His Matie is pleased to declare, *that when he shall have effected what he offers*, his Matie will readily grant him the full benefitt thereof.' Not for Charles II, the leap in the dark.

Other of his subjects were ceaselessly probing at development of auxiliary means important to ships. Francis Smethwick must have 'effected what he offered', since in 1667 Charles gave him

[1] SP16/519/84.   [2] SP44/18/179.

E*

an exclusive 'grant of a new way to grind Optick Glasses, wch will add much to the use of Perspective Glasses at Sea'.[1] An improved telescope was no small advantage in warfare and navigation.

In February '62 we have an attractive appointment to the King's service: 'Our Will and Pleasure is for the [immediate] swearing of Joseph Moxon Our servant, as Hydrographer unto Us for the making of Globes, Mapps and Sea Platts [charts], and that he receive all Profitts and Advantages in as ample manner, as any of Our servants.'[2]

But more attractive than the appointment—enchanting in fact —is the petition that preceded it: 'We your Ma[ties] Loyal Subjects, being most of us Professors of the Mathematics, doe testifie that Joseph Moxon hath made good Globes, Mapps, Sea Platts etc. And that we know of none other in England that makes Globes, but him selfe. And therefore humbly conceive that [his appointment] will be very advantageous to Navigation, and other Mathematical Studies.'[3]

This high testimony is followed by fourteen names of which the last, endearingly, is Euclid Speidell, and the first, I. Newton, D.D.

[1] SP44/25/5.   [2] SP44/45/116.   [3] SP29/49/31.

VI

THE GREAT CIVIL SERVANT

By the shattering evidence of his secret journal, by correspondence and other records, this man has been microscopically viewed by history. Around every corner of the Papers, likewise, we meet him at first hand in his purely professional life with a vividness hardly short of his living presence.

Of mean family, that is, of people who sound greedy and unloving—his family obligations were met not through affection, but through an irritable sense of what was owing to his own dignity—he faithfully deployed the greed and acquisitiveness that had been defeated in them, and added embellishments of his own. Physically he seems to represent a type not uncommon, going by his resemblance to the bulbous-nosed male effigy of the Skynner monument in Ledbury, Herefordshire, if one mentally deprives Skynner of his beard. Dignified in his official capacity, sanctimonious and righteous behind his lecheries actual or wishfully dwelt on, he posed a greater enigma formerly than today, when the idea that in one person live a hundred persons, admirable and despicable, is generally received. The enigma of Samuel Pepys would seem to consist not of his contradictory nature but of his talents—comprehensible least of all by his antecedents. In this Secretary of the Principal Officers of the Navy, capable of marking down a pretty woman whose officer-husband was at sea and committing rape upon her, was also an exquisite perception of beauty, a love of learning, and a gift for order—creative order— so great that it amounted to genius.

The business that passed through his hands included all shipyard contracts, of all kinds whatever. He had to be abreast of current market prices of every commodity to prevent overcharging, and foresee market trends in periods of war and peace. He had to comment intelligently on the quality of hemp, anchors, tallow, timber, canvas and tar; merely knowing what experts to consult on these, in default of his own first-hand knowledge, was in itself a voluminous achievement. The strikes, quarrels and higher-echelon jealousies of every shipyard in England beat ceaselessly upon him. The cry of money shortage and inability to meet payrolls hammered him year in, year out. He was constantly in touch with disputes pending in the Admiralty Courts. He dealt with excuses, alibis and lies in bewildering variety. He visited the shipyards regularly and knew the running expenses of ships under construction, sharply rebuking Christopher Pett for extravagance over the royal yacht itself: *Wee wonder much to heare of* [expense] *for carved worke on the new yaugh: when it was ordered that all carved worke was to bee forborne untill tryall had been made of her sayling.* On top of these staggering professional obligations he was leading a life of his own, crowded with friendships, the intense pleasure of his growing material possessions and social status, a passionate interest in music and the theatre, furtive adulteries with his wife's servant-girls, and high intellectual interests.

From his appointment in 1661 as Secretary to the Navy Office, his first job was to bring order out of the chaotic Naval wreckage left by the Protectorate. This by courtesy would be the joint accomplishment of the Navy Board that he served; by every factual evidence, the special drive and impetus behind the Board were his. Astounding not only is the fact, but the speed with which he did it. That one single man with no prestige of nobility or rank could so impose his influence on six demoralized and bankrupt shipyards within a year seems impossible, but the evidence stands in the Papers. For one letter addressed by beset Naval employees to his colleagues, fifty are addressed to Mr Secretary—not in deference to his position, for there were officers above him, but with an obvious feeling that he was *the* officer to consult in times of trouble, and that his was the final word from which there was no appeal.

The first and most dramatic evidence of the enormous power that the King's instinct for able men had placed in the hands of Samuel Pepys is the abrupt shrinking of the ancient Naval bugbear—the stealing that went on derisively in spite of every effort against it. To say it disappeared is too roseate a statement, but its immediate reduction was conspicuous in all shipyards. He clamped an iron hand on thievery of all kinds; nothing was too small to escape him, and by some occult grapevine an awareness of this penetrated the shipyard complex, down to the meanest intelligence in it. The minuteness of the surveillance was astonishing. When a boatswain in the *Elias* sold some rope, suspicious eyes fastened on him at once and explanations were demanded. The man would have been in trouble if his captain had not been able to attest that the rope did in fact belong to him, and not to the ship. That a transaction so small could not be completed without attracting notice speakes volumes for the efficiency of the system.

The new severity, moreover, inspired shipyard officials to pursue thieves as never before; even if this zeal were to curry favour, it was all to the good. 'I went to pickle hering near Horseydowne',[1] Captain Hickes begins a report to Pepys, the herring being a blind for his real objective—a cache of stolen iron which he had traced in this general direction. Like many another detective he went to the village pub to hear what gossip he could, and struck pay dirt immediately. 'The publicans daughter she sayd that Mr Craft a broken ironmonger hath a whole roome full of Iron Shott; I doe believe this Crafts storehouse is the Gulph that swallows up all.' Beside discovering the receiver, focal point of all organized stealing, he has found a thief who had got this far with a basket of nails and happened to drop it within sight of two women. 'They helped him pick up the nailes,' the report of Hickes continues, 'he saying Good woemen make hast or else I am undone.' The man's abject terror, even at this remove from the yard, advertises the lowest echelon's awareness of the new administration—a contrast with the carefree days when prize ships were handed out right and left like so many wafers.

[1] SP29/V79.

After tightening his grasp on embezzlement, Pepys appears to have given shipyard chiefs rather liberal powers of punishment. He himself apparently had power to issue warrants of arrest and even of distraint, as a request of July '65 indicates.[1] By further allusion of the Papers his next step was a complete overhaul of every financial department within provenance of the Navy, with particular emphasis on the methods of book-keeping employed. 'Inclosed are Accts of Canvas and Cordage,' writes a put-upon storekeeper, 'wch for the most part are entered promiscuously in our books. After a tedious time in abstracting all such petty p'ticulars I was weary and willing to lay it aside' in the hope that the old methods would be resumed; 'but,' he sighs, 'being otherwise informed, I have don it by the present method.'[2] Similar moans and complaints from other clerks were as effective—so far as Pepys was concerned—as chipping at an iceberg.

His most stringent regulations, however, were reserved for pursers. These men, who handled all finances of the ship in which they served, naturally had unequalled opportunities for peculation, which over the centuries they had brought to a fine art. Who, for example, was to disprove their figures showing victuals and beer lost through spoilage, which actually had been pilfered from stores and sold? Accordingly he jumped on the brotherhood by reviving the process of bonding them[3]—an innovation of the Commonwealth's in 1652 against the widespread and ruinous crookedness of Naval pursers, for all the legend of 'Puritan incorruptibility'; but enforced by Pepys with a rigidity previously unknown, to judge by the results. Only on certificate of the Navy Office that his books were clean might the purser reclaim his bond, under the following form of release: ———, *purser of his Ma*[ts] *ship the* ——— *is given this certificate to take up his Bond, entered into for due p'formance of his Duty.* One year later (1664) appears evidence that Pepys had once more followed Commonwealth precedent in allowing pursers, unable to put up the bond, to furnish securities, but first the financial standing of those securities was rigidly investigated: 'I have made inquiry about those persons hereafter mencioned as Securite for William Johnson

[1] SP29/126/18.   [2] SP29/78/106.   [3] SP29 V68 62-63.

purser of his Ma^{ts} ship the *Portland*; I find they are persons of good repute, adiudged sufficient securite for Three Hundred Pounds.'[1]

Having handcuffed the pursers, Mr Secretary moved up to ship's commanders, the only others aboard with unquestioned access to ship's funds. These he shackled by the ruling 'that noe Comander order the payment of any money, unless such Demand bee first attested by the Comand^r and Maister of ye Shipp'[2] that requested the loan. The commander is even forbidden to lend his ships for any service whatsoever, unless by similar attestation of the borrower. From the mountain of old pay-books scanned by Pepys in 1662 come these provisions, and a reference still earlier shows his irritable sense of the money that drains away through small holes: *Captain Tettersell to bee chided for sending a letter by expresse, unnecessarily.*

Contractors and suppliers to the Navy palpably had confidence in his fairness, complaining freely of yard favoritism and the like; on the other hand Pepys, while consistently equitable, never gave them an inch of leeway. Captain Alleyn of Chatham ropeyard explains distractedly that the debris called 'ground towes and rakeings of the yard'[3] cannot be estimated separately as Pepys has commanded, 'they all lying promiscuously together for want of roome'; for this reason Mr Waterhouse, who buys up such trash, has had the rakings thrown in with the ground tows, but explains that he doesn't want the rakings anyway. Pepys had been afraid the junkman was getting too good a bargain at the Navy's expense; even the leavings of a ropeyard were not beneath his notice.

In writing to personages royal or noble, undoubtedly Pepys displayed all the courtly humility and deference proper to their rank. Far more interesting is the manner of his communication with equals and subordinates between 1661-65. These were the years of his first taste of power, and his behaviour was exactly that of every power-hungry man; at first ruthlessly authoritarian, then later—the hunger full-fed—considerably mellower. Of this life-pattern his earlier business correspondence gives the initial and symptomatic beginnings.

With upper officials of shipyards, or of any Naval department,

[1] SP29/91/14.   [2] SP29/88/31.   [3] SP29/132/18.

he was far too clever to parade his authority or insist on it. To Pett, Furzer and the like he begins his letters, *I would desire you to do thus and so*, and signs himself *Your affect^ate freind*. They on their side addressed him with proper respect but no hint of subservience; the tone of equality is patent. Phineas in particular never minced words when displeased. 'I understand not what you meane by your long silence,' he begins waspishly on one occasion. 'Great things are commanded to be done here, but having not the least assistance from you, is to make bricks without straw.'[1] Still less does he modify his style when explaining that he has plenty of tree-nails on hand, 'therefore desire you would forbeare medling with them'.[2] Yet however crusty his letters, he never fails of sending best wishes to Mrs Pepys—indicating that the families knew each other socially as well as professionally.

As for Mr Secretary's relations with inferior officers of ships and shipyards, there are no two ways about it. By their letters to him, and by his answers, it is clear that with these lower ranks he felt no need to observe the caution he observed with their superiors. First of all he never—or virtually never—wrote directly to such personnel; upon their letters he jotted two or three words from which his clerks could frame replies. If this is routine for a man overburdened with correspondence, nothing else about it is routine; from his attitude toward his subordinates one might deduce their attitude toward him, if deduction were needed. Since we have their own voices, testifying at first-hand, no such need arises.

Their approach to him was as obsequious and grovelling as his to them was harsh, peremptory and overbearing in the last degree. Neither criticism nor condonation enter into what seems the mere fact: they were terrified of him. Nowhere in the Papers are other Principal Officers, such as the eminent Sir John Mennes, addressed with similar dread and propitiation; a thousand examples could be cited. 'I make bould to give ye Trouble, humbly Craveinge you will bee pleased to excuse me cumming to London at p'sent. truly it will bee a great hinderance to me to take ye Journey at this time,'[3] plus further agonized contortions of excuse.

[1] SP29/98/124.   [2] SP29/100/127.   [3] SP29/56/115.

Beneath these writhings Pepys has written: *Order him upp.* 'By a great oversight in me,' a purser supplicates, 'ye gunners mate was left out of my pay books. I humbly crave yr hon^rs ffavour; it was only an oversight in mee and noe defraude unto his Majestye. I humbly beg yr pardon'[1]—the sort of appeal to rouse Mr Secretary's utmost scepticism if not worse; suppressing a name in a paybook meant part of the man's pay in the purser's pocket, plus the value of his victuals. 'I crave yr hon^rs pardon,' other crawling apologies begin, the most nervous and abject of them for delay in submitting accounts, something Pepys hated particularly. Even Phineas, when asking a favour, begins cautiously, 'I intreate'; even the doughty Mydleton begs pardon for taking emergency cable without order. Heavy upon all ranks hung the same desire for his approval, the same anxiety to keep on the right side of him.

Heavy on Pepys, on the other hand, hung the ruined Navy that had to be recreated in all its thousand aspects; if he vented the nervous strain of it on those who could not talk back, it is probable that he suspected them *en masse* of having a share in the ruin. He knew all about the huge thefts in ships and shipyards and knew also that the workmen and petty officers were chiefly responsible for it, and was prepared to show them they had an ugly customer to deal with. He hauled up before him the artisans whose quarrels wasted the time the King was paying for, and with those lethal jottings of his made short work of them: *Mr Hall Anchorsmith to have Six weekes and not longer, to make good his Contracte.*

Some letters written in the six-month period between September '65 and February '66 display a tense moment in the famous Pepys-Evelyn friendship—a lesion that must have been painful while it lasted. Precisely what aberration led a man of John Evelyn's calibre to be appointed a Commissioner for War Prisoners, is as baffling as the aberration that led him to accept it. Patriotic duty undoubtedly moved him—the desire to do what he could when other men were fighting and dying. All the same, for a man of Evelyn's nature—gentle, sensitive, happiest when absorbed in the science of trees and gardens, vulnerable through over-refinement of feeling and religious scruple—no job could have been

[1] SP29/68.

more lethally unsuitable. Faced with the infections and stench of thousands of Dutch prisoners, faced with the scandalous shortages of food, shelter and clothing that were killing them off at the rate of some fifty a week regularly, he could do little for his torment but be vocal about it to Pepys. On a lower key J. V. Hosier, another Commissioner, was vocal likewise: 'Ye Prisoners dye Comonly 3 or 4 in A day; there is noe finding out their names. I am informed they are to be allowed for ye future, nothing but Bread and Water; if soe, it is not possible for them to live one weeke longer.'[1]

If Hosier, a much more stolid character, were shaken, Evelyn's demoralized entreaties to Pepys show how completely unable he was to bear it. 'Sir, of the 5,000 lib I was to have this weeke, no lesse than 3,000 is diverted for other purposes. Consider the misery and confusion at Chatham if I doe not send this monneye; dreadfull will be the consequence . . .'[2] Without monneys I cannot feed two-thousand prisoners; my arreares at Chatham are soe greate, that I dare not shew them my face. . . .'[3] Our barbarous exposure of ye prisoners to the utmost of sufferings must needs redound to his Ma[ties] great dishonour . . . I am almost in despaire, soe you will pardon my passion.'[4]

His nightmare was solaced occasionally by episodes such as the King's visit to 'our Infirmary at Chatham,' he writes, 'wch his Ma[tie] gave me leave to explaine to him at large [at length]'.[5] He then begs Pepys to recommend the Infirmary to the Duke, which emphasizes the Secretary's direct access to royalty, and his power to get backing from them.

But such alleviations, for Evelyn, were brief; the darkening and thickening nightmare reclaimed him. Both by word and by inference it is plain that he hounded Pepys incessantly for money and that Pepys, with no money to give, reacted as people do to this pressure—by exploding more or less. Evelyn's letter of self-defence combines, with the dignity one might expect of him, all the power of unresentful and gentlemanly reproach: 'Sir, I doe not set you these stories out of desire to trouble you, as you have

---

[1] SP29/137/74.   [2] SP29/133.   [3] SP29/134/23.   [4] SP29/133/63-I
[5] SP29/148/51.

lately seem'd to impute to me; that I have made Complaints is not
at all my crime. I shall be most tender to yr burthen, wch is
already insupportable, but I beseache you to believe I have not
exaggerated mine Owne Sufferings. Be pleased to look upon me,'
he concludes on a note of exhausted submission, 'as a plaine Man
who desires to serve his Matie, till he is pleased to release me.'[1] The
brief estrangement, happily, did no permanent harm to their
relationship.

The episode of hidden gold in the Tower, too famous, even now
pins the attention at sight of Charles's own warrant authorizing
the search: 'Whereas Wee are given to understand that there lyes
hid in ye Tower of London, or in ye Hamlett thereunto ad-
joining, a quantity of Gold and Silver originally belonging to Us;
Our Will is that you make diligent and exact search—'[2] which,
according to J. T. Quarrell's delightful book BURIED TREASURE,
was in the wrong place altogether. But the Tower gold that
eluded the diggers perhaps turned up—for one person—in a
second royal warrant empowering the same quest. The King had
any number of officers to whom he could have entrusted the search,
yet from among them all he chose the man so obscure by birth,
so unknown till recently, naming him as 'Our trusty and well
beloved Servant, Samuel Pepys Esquire',[3] the pleasure of the
formulary *trusty and well beloved* perhaps eclipsed by the burnish-
ment—the aureate gloss—of *Esquire*.

[1] SP29/134/23.   [2] SP29/109/4.   [3] SP29/109/5.

VII

CURIOSITIES

THE Pandora's Box that holds the world of vanished Naval affairs holds likewise myriad fragments associated indirectly with the Navy—a shifting mass in which separate particles pick up the light for an instant before vanishing into darkness and separate voices claim the ear before vanishing into silence. Out of this conglomerate dust appear grotesque beings and situations, oddities and obscurities unrelated yet stemming—however obscurely —from the King's ships.

Foremost among the living figures who pass briefly before us are sea-captains: not in their conventional dignity of command, but in aspects less imaginable. There was the brilliant young Captain John Pennington (a cousin of the Admiral?) who lay dying in his London lodging, as deposed by his landlord in 1632: 'Hee was ill at ease about 3 weeks but kept not his chamber above 3 days. On the ffriday night hee, looking somewhat wildly, asked what was that little black thing that lay nibling at his feete? Then falling into a Convulsion shutt his eyes, and never opened them againe till the very instant hee gave up the Ghost.'[1] Or take Captain Richard Beach and his salty attack on the Navy Office: 'I understand that my Master Nath. Southwood hath Informed Yo that I have Strocke him; he ran the Ship aground and ther she Laye for 2 houres. I tould him hee did not worcke Lyke a Seaman to gett her off againe; hee telling me I knew nothing, I did Stricke him over the pate with my cane; and shall doe the Lyke to any Shall give mee such Landgage; and desire you to send mee one that will not be druncke with Eavery idle fellow.'[2] But even this

---

[1] SP16/230/81.   [2] SP29/159/61.

forthright mariner pales beside the dazzling Captain Lydall of the *Roebuck*. 'He comes on shoare, and never goes on board night nor day,' reports John Gordier of Plymouth, justifiably shocked. 'And tell him of the danger, he sayes the Navy Officers may (saving yr presence) kisse his Arse, hee will observe noe orders, not hee. Hee carrys an Instrument of Musique by a boy, up and downe the Towne; and leads ye gentlemens Sonnes to ill houses.'[1] After this brilliant original we may admire the more conventional Captain Talbot and his ship the *Elizabeth*, the man and the ship both reported hurt in recent battle, but no; the *Elizabeth* sails nonchalantly into Aldborough, and the captain can be seen 'walking the decke in his silke morning gown'.[2]

In stirring up at hazard this huge rubble of ancient bygones, a few whiffs of skulduggery float upward—faint but undeniable, circuitously expressed, and mostly remarkable for the fact that any mention of them, at all, should be committed to writing. The prize exhibit is certainly a letter of January 16, 1629, and from the highest of all sources—Charles I's Principal Secretary, Nicholas, to Abraham Davies, official receiver of prize ships and cargo: 'My Lady Duches [of Buckingham] hath desired me to entreate you [for] a note of all prize shippes and goods and wreckes, brought in, and as neere an estimat as may bee, of the true vallew of such goodes. *By this you will do his Ma^ty good Service; the more privatt you are herein, the better.*'[3]

The situation behind the letter is that Buckingham, assassinated a year ago, had severely damaged his wife's huge estate by his extravagance, and the Duchess now found herself swamped by his debts. Part of the Duke's pay, perhaps most part, had been his Droits (perquisites) of Lord High Admiral—his right to captured ships, cargo and wrecks. With his death such rights had automatically ceased, yet in this single case, by the King's own desire (*by this you will doe his Ma^ty good Service*) the established order was evaded and the widow was obviously going to be allowed a share of Droits one year after both her husband and her husband's right had expired. Obviously likewise the King, out of love for Buckingham and knowledge of what he had done for the Navy,

---

[1] SP29/197/95.   [2] SP29/165/80.   [3] SP14/215/81.

was conniving at an improper and illegal transaction (*the more privatt you are herein, the better*). Connivance and collusion usually carry a taint of some kind, but by the universal law of exceptions this collusion seems justifiable, even admirable.

Something of more sinister depth, and far more unplumbed, was the suicide of the Lord Warden of the Cinque Ports, darkly alluded to in a letter of March, 1618, from one John Castle: 'Yf the Spanyardes had come, wee might have had our throats cut full well. for hee sent downe a great manie Barrells of Powder to Dovor Castle, and they proved nothinge but Sande, with a little Powder upon the Toppe of them.'[1] How explain this supreme treachery? And had authority begun getting wind of it? If so, there was no way out for the Lord Warden but the one he took.

Of all imaginable purlieus for obscurities and suppressions the Admiralty Court is least imaginable, but undeniably there exists an instruction 'to unlade and examine the shipp called the *Golden Herring; the ground of this order, for reasons of State, not fitt to be published*'.[2] Pursuit of the *Herring* clarifies this hugger-mugger only dubiously. The ship was an Amsterdam merchantman taken as prize 'by his Maties ffleete and brought about to London', the owners petition. 'And since that tyme many of the goods are pillaged and carried away out of her, and more dayly like to bee ymbeaslled.'[3] One conjectural reason for keeping the case dark is that the Admiralty Court, guarding its high reputation as impartial judge for seamen and merchants of all nations, considered it so grossly scandalous that a ship under its seal could be looted in this fashion, that it suppressed the facts for the sake of its own credit.

Unexpectedly the shipyards, with their workmen's brawls raging undisguised under the open sky, contribute a double mystery of theft and murder. A worker at Chatham yard, one Woodcott, is discovered to have stolen a good deal of cash; just as they go to arrest him, he vanishes. Yet all his possessions remain in his home, and manifestly his disappearance is not a mere matter of flight. Searchers tear his house apart looking for the money, but:

[1] SP14/107/23.   [2] SP16/52/46.   [3] SP16/42/121 122.

'Wee find nothing Considerable,' they report, 'to make satisfaction for such moneys as was retained by him.'[1] Days pass, neither Woodcott nor the money is ever seen again, and authority is forced to admit, 'What more is to be don in it, we know not'. The unavoidable conclusion is Woodcott's murder by his unknown confederates, either for his refusal to share the loot, or to disclose its hiding-place. If the theory is tenable, it may be that somewhere near Chatham two objects await discovery, an anonymous skeleton and a cache of silver coin; a large one, to judge by the vigour and persistence of the search for it.

'Flotsam, jetsam, ligan, deodands and drifts; treasure trove, fishes royal and ambergris.' These beautiful words, scattered throughout the Papers like shells on a beach, boil down to one thing: salvage. Hungry eyes constantly watched the sea, alert for any floating object whatever; nothing was too inconsiderable to precipitate bloody fights on shore and foul words and threats shouted from boat to boat as they raced toward a wreck. The whole curious subject of salvage is feverish with strife, with greedy hands snatching, and with the peculiarly poignant rage of human cormorants compelled to disgorge what they had swallowed.

The booty of the sea had to be defined and re-defined a hundred times over in order to bring, to this ferocious conflict of sharks, some semblance of law and order. For example, at what precise point did a disabled ship become, technically, a wreck? A ruling of 1621 replies: when six or seven tides have washed over her when stranded or aground, she shall be considered a wreck. Yet with poor fishermen seeing from some lonely shore a cargo vessel stuck on a reef, it requires an effort of imagination to conceive them as waiting punctiliously for the correct number of tides to pass. Another ruling on wrecks is iron-bound: there must be no living thing on board. One Peter Jagowe, claiming his share of a 'flemish bottome' is careful to specify that 'wee found neither man, boye, dog nor Catt aboard'. But about the same time

[1] SP29/147/78.

a wrecked ship laden with Nantes wines looked like a wreck till they got there—and found in her a living dog. Over the immediate uproar of conflicting claims peals the decision of Sir George Harmon who says that 'the ship derelict, having a dog alive in her, does not belong to the Lord Warden of the Cinque Ports, but to the owners'. Did the owners deliberately leave the poor creature aboard, as one leaves a magazine to prove possession of a seat? If true, the proof held firm—but not firm enough to defeat the Lord Warden's claim to twenty-five per cent of the wines, which he got. Another inventive salvage grab was the stipulation: 'Any Ship running aground within the Admiraltie of the Cinque Ports, forfeits her best Anchor and Cable'.

The value of wreck, obviously, could be anything. Ten per cent of all gold or silver 'taken up out of the sea' was the King's right, but if the looters had got there first the King's right might be purely technical. By a provision of 1616, illicit plunderers could be punished by the mayor of the port 'provided the ship could be reached on horseback, at low water'—frail barrier against the hordes waiting to swoop. Unavoidably slower off the mark, but not far behind, came the local bigwigs determined, with no less ferocity, to get their bite out of whatever was going. Yet there exist evidences of compromise (1618): warrants that call on looters to 'deliver up' what they have pillaged, as well as other warrants that authorize 'compounding with the savers'—a politic step, in view of the sort of resistance they would meet in trying to get it all back.

A more gruesome companion to the solitary dog was a Hamburg merchantman boarded by pirates in May or June, 1637, 'which after they had pillaged her, cutt 2 great holes in her syde to sink her, but beinge laden with Oyls it bore upp the ship, and winds putt her ashore at Seaford' in July. At once boats put out from Seaford—without mention of tidal etiquette—and found in her 'a dead man with his head shott off; by his state it appears that the ship had driven long at sea'—a crazy wandering Ophelia of the deep, her other passengers murdered or captured for the slave trade. The Seaford people took some bales of silk out of her; the next high water washed her still further ashore, and they saved more bales. At once the Lord Warden claimed the salvaged goods, and with equal promptness the salvagers petitioned for 'one halfe the vallew, according to former usage', claiming that 'with great peril of their lives they saved goods to the worth of £2,000 out of the ship'. One hopes they got it; the Admiralty Court Archives would provide the answer.

A cargo of money—such cargoes seeming rather frequent—naturally touched off the most incendiary disputes of all. In March, 1637, a Spanish ship with much gold and silver aboard was wrecked off the Isle of Wight, noted long ago (and sourly) as 'very rich in such perquisites'. The instant fight over the precious freight was dominated by the equally-instant pronouncement that 'a good part is already adjudged to his Ma^{ty}', and the Vice-Admiral of the Island is claiming his fifty per cent. One savage footnote of these battles, identical to Naval or commercial wrecks, disturbed no one but a few people too civilized for their own good. In a 'miserable wreck' at Bosheston in January, 1631, all on board perished. 'The dead bodies still lie stript naked upon the rocks and sands, unburied.' George Ellis, the Admiralty official reporting this, was the only one upset; the rest were exclusively concerned with getting their claims to London first. Ellis then addressed the Admiralty Court, praying that it might deal with 'the barbarous disorder of pillaging ships wrecked and cast away on the sea-coast'. The answer to his plea for humanity may still be read in the decisive pen-marks that struck it out.

In this matter of bodies cast ashore was the peculiarly frightful possibility—certainly not overlooked by Ellis—that some of them might still have been alive and able to recover; a situation taken care of by looters without loss of time, as in the classic case of Admiral Sir Cloudesley Shovell. Shipwrecked, flung ashore and approached by the hag who discovered him first, tactlessly he began to show signs of life; with the casualness and efficiency that bespoke long experience she dropped a few handsful of sand over his face and unhurriedly stripped him of clothes and jewellery, including the valuable ring that brought her to the gallows.

In 1665 Charles II restated and redefined salvage rights as between the Crown and the Lord High Admiral, 'upon full hearing and debate of the King's Council, and Admiralty Judges'. This provides that 'all [enemy] Shippes and Goods coming into any Port Creeke or Road, by stress of weather or accident; all Enemy Shipps seized by any Vessell not commisionated; All Shipps rescued; all Shipps forsaken; all Shipps pursued by comissionated Shipps',[1] all belong to the Lord High Admiral. The King benefits only when enemy ships are driven into English ports by the King's men-of-war, or by commissioned ships.

Every case of a looted wreck was followed by a spate of instructions for punishing looters. Their very number and variety seem to indicate how powerless they were, above all in well-populated ports, where looters 'disperse them Selfes and cannot be found', as pursuing officials report despondently. Not that the same difficulty obtained in sparsely-settled areas, where the presence of a gold-laced velvet coat or gold ring in a fisherman's hut, or a handsome dress on his wife's back, was betrayal enough. In one rare instance two men were swooped on after a wreck in which the Earl of Desmond was lost: 'David Prythergh a pedlar and his son, founde with one of his L^{ps} trunkes, were committed to gaol.' One year later the gaoler ventures to remind the Admiralty that 'they are still lying there, in grate misery and wante'. In all this cormorant ferocity appears a lesser bone of contention, ambergris; seldom found but always the subject of bitter disputes, whose settlement usually fades into the void. On one Admiralty memorandum is a marginal jotting: *What shall be don touching Mr Carew and his wyfe who are in ye Messengers Custody by their refusall to deliver upp a quantity of ambergreece gathered in Cornwall.*[2] After this a note, *Reference to Mr Attorney*, with no further elucidation, but it looks rather bleak for the Carews.

Among all the Naval torments, cooks were a special torment, then as now in short supply. 'In the ship,' mourns a captain, on the usual elegiac note, 'I have but one smale youth to dress victualls.' Like all those lower ranks called 'subordinate ministers to the Navie', cooks took an oath:

[1] SP29/150/56.   [2] SP16/215/98.

'You shall sweare That you will behave your selfe honestly in your place, as Cooke of his Ma^tys Ship ye ———. You shall use noe deceitfull or fraudulent course in dressing the Companies vittles, by pricking ye Beefe or Porke whilst it is in boyling, to let out ye fatt, nor otherwise wrong the same in quantity or goodnes. You shall not purloine any part thereof but use your best skill for ye use of men serving his Matie, so helpe you god.'

Yet a conscientious cook might serve up poor food through no fault of his own. Thomas Allen, an official inspector of meat supply in 1673, saw inferior beef being cut up and protested 'to the clerk of the cutting-house, that it would make but little bruish [gravy] for the seamen and little fat for the cook. He replied, it was good enough for the price.' From other vistas of time is borne to us the plaint of a ship's cook, John Attewell, in gaol for debt; he is not allowed to have his own bed there but 'is forced to lye uppon boardes, with pease straw'. So scarce an article as a ship's cook was more useful in his galley than repining on pease straw, and the Lords of Admiralty got him out shortly afterward.

In this swirling eddy of fragments animate and inanimate, some peripheral flotsam is not least fascinating—faces and voices in faint aftermath, people not directly connected with the Navy but with those who, in their day, had power to affect the Navy for good or ill. Easily heading the list in the Papers, by mere quantity of allusion, are Cromwell's elder son Richard and the widow of the 'Protector' himself. Bearers of a name that must have been anathema in many circles, they cannot sufficiently obscure themselves, but willy-nilly are thrust into conspicuousness again with Richard, erstwhile Protector, getting by far the worst of it. This mild, well-meaning and singularly unfortunate man has fled to France even before the Restoration. Not for fear of the King's vengeance—for Charles, characteristically, showed no disposition to lift a finger against any surviving Cromwell—but for fear of the huge menace forever overhanging him, the £20,000 for his father's State funeral, of which not one penny has ever been paid. In 1665, however, with the Dutch War imminent and the French hostile, the King by proclamation has recalled all English residents from France. At once Richard petitions urgently to be exempted from this order, since on his return to England 'his debts would ruine him'. He protests moreover that far from heading any new Puritan rising, as has been rumoured, he is leading an absolutely retired and harmless life.

In support of Richard's statement a family servant in the employ of his wife Dorothy, one William Mumford, makes a deposition before a JP at Westminster in March '65. 'Hee [Richard] is forced to write his wife under cover of a Baker in Ayre Street Pickadilly, the contents whereof was complaints for money; that hee doth not [communicate] with any ffanaticks; and that the said Richard Cromwell doth change his name with his dwellings, that hee may keep him selfe unknown.'[1]

Mumford is speaking with authority, since he himself 'hath lived with the said Richard for a twelvemonth in Paris, and his whole occupation there was drawing of landskips [landscapes] and reading of Bookes; and hee saw not any Englishman that whole time'. Mumford now discloses that Richard's sole support is out of his wife's £600 a year, and that 'he is not a sixpence the better for being the son of the pretended protector'. And far from wishing harm to the King, Mumford continues, 'I have often heard him pray in his private prayers for his Matie; and speak often with great Reverence of his Maties Grace and ffavour to himselfe and family, in suffering them to enjoy their lives, and the little fortunes they have'. Unwittingly Mumford depicts a very desolation of exile, sad and furtive; the dodging about from one address to another, the assumed names, the letters written under cover, the avoidance of English company, the unbroken loneliness—every mark of the man afraid not only of being hunted, but even of being noticed.

Richard's mother likewise had had unpleasant moments of her own to live through; very remarkable, in the following document, is the manner in which she dissociates herself from her dead husband Oliver and her living son Richard (1662):

[1] SP29/151/67.

The Humble Petition of Elizabeth Cromwell widowe, sheweth:
'That among her many sorrows, she is unjustly charged of detaining Jewels belonging to Y^r Majestie; wch beside the disrepute of it, hath exposed her to many violences and losses under pretence of searching her abode for such goods; she being willing to depose upon oath that she neither hath nor knowes of any such Jewels. And she hath never intermedled in [anything] wch hath been prejudiciall to Y^r Majesties Royall Father or your Selfe. She therefore humbly prays that your Majestie *would distinguish betwixt herself and those of her relations who have been obnoxious*, and vouchsafe her a protection, without which she cannot expect, in her old age, a safe retirement in any place.'[1]

Remoter still, on more outward-spreading rings of time, floats the face of poor Katherine, the widow of handsome Buckingham. Passionately in love with the living man, passionately loving his memory, for as much as six years after his murder she was still invoking his name as the most powerful talisman she possessed. 'Lett me intrett you to gett a porcers [purser's] plase for one that did norse one of my boyes but sinse is falen into great wante and miserys. For Gorge's sake', she begs in her awful scrawl. 'Doe this for Gorge's sake.'[2] Yet she had been a young woman at his death and inevitably, in seven or eight years, married again. When last heard of in the Papers she is at Tunbridge Wells where her new husband is knocking her fortune to pieces at the gaming table, while Katherine amuses herself by having a miscarriage.

Among so many thousand presences ranging from highest to lowest rank, the presence of downright infamy is creditably rare—and yet, once in a while, its livid face peeps out. Jno. Carlisle, Clerk of Dover Port, obstructs the landing of English seamen released from Dutch prisons and coming home sick, battered and emaciated, till he has exacted tenpence a head from the Dutch commanders bringing them over. This leech on the body of distress is exposed when a Captain Heinsius, who has promised him sixpence a head for the sake of peace, complains to the Admiralty. Carlisle first protests piously that 'hee cannot forgoe all the duties

1 SP29/22/144.   2 SP16/269/43.

for the towne', then even more piously reveals that he has reduced the extortion to fourpence a head, of which '2d will bee for him selfe, and 2d for the water bailiffe'.

At the other extreme shines pure devotion, the light of pure hero-worship. J. A. Hayes, aboard the *Royal Charles* during the battle of June, 1666, is afraid that Prince Rupert will not get his share of credit. 'Since lying Wretches speak dishonorably of the Prince,' he *prints* at his own expense an eye-witness testimonial: 'Never any Prince nor private person was in War exposed to more danger, from beginning to end. His fearless Courage in ye middest of Showers of Cannon bullet carrying him to change his ship three tymes, setting up the Royal Standard in each of them, to animate the Men.'[1] Even the Prince's sloop *Fan-Fan*, built to his order, came in for its share of glory—the tiny craft that rowed boldly up to the Dutch Admiral's flagship and from that position of safety in the very loom of the monster—since the flagship guns could not get low enough to rake her—she sat insolently for one hour, banging away at a target impossible to miss, with the English splitting their sides at the spectacle and one of them bursting into poetry:

> Neptune and Oceanus,
> With all the Sea-borne traine,
> Tuck up your Sea-green Mantles
> & Gallop for the Maine.
> Make all the speede you can,
> To see the ffan-ffann.
> Bellona smil'd upon her
> & breath'd on every man
> Both victory and honour
> Aboard the ffan-ffann.[2]

The supernatural and inexplicable, the mysterious and fanciful, are the last attributes one might expect in relation to the King's ships, with their life of hard facts and harder knocks. Yet by one

[1] SP29/159/3-3-I.   [2] SP29/165/2.

incontrovertible example the English Navy appears in prophecy, and by another in the clouds. 'In 1582 one Paulus Grebnerus (Grebner) visited England and presented Queene Elizabeth with a faire Manuscript in Latine, describing the future history of Europe. Dr Nevil being in favour with the Queene obteined this booke of her and bestowed it on the Library of Trinity College in Cambridge, where it hath been published [exposed] to the view of all persons till slurred and defaced by much perusing and ill-handling.'[1] The prophecy reads, in part:

'About 1649 a Northerne Kinge should reigne, Charles by Name, who shall take to wife Mary of the Popish Religion, from whych time he shalbe a most unfortunate Prince. Then the People of the Dominion shall chuse another Governor, viz, an Earle, and afterwards another Commander, viz, a Knight, not of the same family or Dignity; who shall trample all under his feet. And after him shall appeare one Charles descending from Charles, with a mighty Navy on the Shore of his Fathers Kingdome.'

The manuscript is still in Trinity College Library under the class-mark *Grebneri Vaticinia, Given by Nevile*. Grebner's visit to England, which Nevill dates as in 1582, appears on the original as 1585, the presentation to Elizabeth not being until 1586. This chillingly exact forecast of events sixty-three and seventy-three years in the future, fourteen years before the birth of Charles I and forty-three years before that of Charles II, must be one of the most authentic fulfilled prophecies in existence.

The navy in the clouds was seen at Newcastle on July 27, 1666. 'About 6 in the afternoone, riding at Shields, being come on decke we did se very visibly the Clouds shewing 3 or 4 ships. Then disappeared in a great Smoke, and in the Smoke perfectly to be seen a great ship without masts. Then suddenly appeared a flete of ships very desserrable [discernible] the greatest of them her hull, masts, yards, top gallant mast very perfectly reproduced as any ship in the harbour, lying very much along on [her side] as if sinking. And this I can attest as a truth.' This might have been a

[1] SP18/I/101.

mirage of one of the countless scattering sea-fights during this period of the Dutch War, and ignorance and credulity do not seem to figure in this careful description of a phenomenon that went on for some time. Nor did universal ignorance and credulity prevail during the period; plenty of contemporary evidence proves the existence of hard-headed men who observed things in a spirit of scientific detachment—not the great minds like Newton's only, but quite ordinary people's. For example in June, 1666, at Aldborough, the sea turned red for miles, and naturally the common report was blood, delicious thrill. But unfortunately 'an ingenious surgeon has examined it, and declares it to be the spawn of fish'—an unkind blow to the horror-mongers.

More chilling even than prophecies and phantom ships is a prophecy unrecognized then but lethally fulfilled before our living eyes, in an Admiralty Court petition of June '64—a creeping fuse that will explode into the ruins and despairs of the American Civil War two hundred years later, and into other endless ruin for our own time. The Company of Royal Adventurers in Africa beg for Naval convoy, since 'they have received the most Insolent protests from the Holland Consul at Castco de Mina, interdicting them to trade at all on that Coast'.[1] In plain terms they advance their strongest argument for obtaining convoy: that their African trade has been chiefly 'for Y^r Ma^{tys} American plantations, *which must necessarily fall through the want of Negro-sarvants*'. It is the slave-trade for which they request Naval protection, though the opprobrious term itself is tactfully omitted.

When war was a gentleman's province, certain courtesies were as rigidly prescribed as in a drawing-room. On a day of 1627 a Holland fleet passed Deal Castle without striking its flag. The Captain of the Castle, William Byng, put a shot across the Admiral's bows to remind him of his duty. The flag was struck. Byng now had himself rowed out to the flagship and demanded, 'as the custom is', to be paid for the shot. The Admiral offered him the equivalent in gunpowder; Byng politely waived the payment; the Admiral tipped Byng's rowers, and all parted on the happiest terms. Equally urbane were the courtesies observed when France

[1] SP29/90/83.

had joined the Dutch in the war against England in 1667, yet in June of that year a French ship sailed into Plymouth with a cargo of French wines, 'a present from the Duc de Vermeuil to King Charles,' and got a special warrant to unlade them. On the reverse of the medal are Naval captures of a non-lethal kind, that make up in malice what they lack in bloodshed: Captain Austin holds up two Flemings with a cargo of oysters and detains them 'Untill their Oysters begann to die'; then he let them go.

The tale of escaping prisoners dashes headlong through the Papers as records of fact plus orders to pursue. Captives of every kind—runaways from Naval impressment, English prisoners of war in prisons overseas—were constantly breaking out or trying to, but the end of these tales remains mostly obscure. One complete story of escape, however, does survive in our source: a hair-raising exploit possible only to seamen who were virtual acrobats, capable of swarming up tall masts in every condition of violent rain, wind and tempest-driven angles. The narrative of Zachary Ewell, prisoner of war in Holland, is electric with the reckless and desperate courage of the escapers, even though what he relates must have come to him by prison grapevine:

'Nine of our men brake out of prison in the night. with crooked nayles they pikt the lockes, got out oppon one another Shoulders and mounted up to the top of a high house. and with a String [rope] made of spliced and pieced canvis, haled [hauled] up one another, and running over the tops of the houses fastened the String to a Chimney and slid and tumbled downe into the street. But the tyles of the house shattring Allarmed the Street, yet they got clear away.'[1]

The steeply-pitched roofs of old Amsterdam rise in the mind as he speaks, with men running along the narrow roof-trees, like rope-walkers in the dark. Ewell then tells how the Dutch are

[1] SP29/137/130.

F

taking it out on the ones who are left: 'Wee remayning have suffered deeply, ffeatred [fettered] with Irons and Chayned all together with Inhuman and Barbrous usage, kept close prisoners in noysome dungeons.' He identifies himself as a licensed pilot of Trinity House and 'a younger brother of that corporation', and subscribes himself 'from the Doalfull, dreadfull and deathly prison, the Princes Haft, in Amsterdam'.

Kidnappings and a Trial

Both time and the ocean, capriciously swallowing things without trace, yield up with equal caprice the secrets hidden in them. One such waterlogged fragment drifts to the surface from the year 1636; a forgotten story opened by a letter from Captain Giles Penn to Buckingham's secretary, Nicholas: 'The heathen Moors of Sallee [Barbary] who for many years have been taking English ships and selling crews into slavery, *are now kidnapping women and children* (writer's italics).'

The skeleton suggestion of this extended slave-trade takes on flesh with the account of the *Little David*, a London ship carrying fifty men, boys and women to Virginia in 1635. The ship was captured by Barbary pirates who took it to Algiers and sold the passengers and crew. The captain of the *Little David*, one John Dunton, was bought by a palpably sharp businessman named Ali Golant. The moment this opportunist realized that Dunton could take entire charge of a ship, he forced him—in Dunton's own words—'to go pylot to the English Channel *for taking Englishwomen, being of more worth than other*'. The sinister allusion to value brings up an image of Englishwomen exposed for sale in the slave-market. More sinister still is Dunton's virtual statement that there existed a regularly organized service for supplying Englishwomen to those markets; and even if the chief victims were women being transported to the colonies in convict hulks, the picture is not much softened.

The secret traffic would have remained secret if not for one of those violent accidents common to the tale of seas. The ship that Dunton was piloting for his Algerian master was herself captured by an English ship carrying Jerome, Admiral Lord Portland.

Dunton, taken prisoner, was brought before the Admiral. Portland examined him and others of the crew at Winchester on
September 28, 1636, and sent their depositions to the Admiralty
with the terse comment, 'If they shall confesse as much att tryall
as they have done heere, I presume there will need noe other
evidence against them'.

Now English justice, which can exhibit trials to its shame,
exhibits one of those trials which are its glory.[1] 'Whereas order
is given . . . to call a Sessions for tryall of certaine Moores or
Turkes lately brought in,' begins the first warrant, dated October,
1636, so they were certainly losing no time.

In the same month the whole crew were tried at Winchester;
among the Moors were four 'renagadoe Dutchmen', i.e., Moslem
converts. The prisoners had a very fair trial and a good jury.
Eleven of the Moors were condemned 'of murder and piracy,
and sentenced to death'. The defence of one—that he did not
intend to kill anyone he took, only to sell them as slaves—seems
to have been coldly received. 'Two of them,' report the Minutes,
with manifest contempt, 'offered to be Christians.' But among the
condemned 'are 2 yonge men not above 13 or 14 yeares of age'.
The English obviously hate the idea of executing them, and
there are some who think 'they may be made good Christians'.
Since a child of fourteen was to be burned for heresy at the
vigorous instance of good Bishop Bonner, and since children
were hanged for petty theft in England up to the nineteenth
century, this early compunction is especially soothing and
grateful.

Throughout the trial Dunton's name is entirely, and strangely,
absent; this cannot but suggest that he deliberately allowed his
ship to be captured by Portland. The acquittal of the four Moslem
Dutchmen implies, similarly, that their conversions as well as their
kidnapping activities were matters of duress. All the same they
had a fair prospect of being hanged, and upon the favourable
verdict—as they lined up before the judge to receive their freedom,
laced with harsh admonitions to repentance—the release of ten-
sion was so great that one of them 'fainted and fell down at the

[1] SP16/335/25, I, II.

bar. The sweat run down his face as he fell, by consideration of the foulness of his sin being laid open to him'.

Now, in late October, 1636, the position is still that eleven men are to be strung up. The matter, however, is far from simple; considerations of terrible import stayed the hangman's hand. Hundreds of Englishmen were held in slavery by the Moors and Turks, and the eleven executions—if carried out—were sure to precipitate a wholesale butchery of English slaves by way of reprisal. This is why anxious inquiries kept coming from Winchester to the Admiralty for months after the trial: 'Will Y° L^pps be pleased to give order, what shalbe done with those condempt, whether they shalbe executed, or imployed for Redemption of Captives.' Exchange of Moors for English slaves certainly made better sense than eleven Moors hanged in England and countless Englishmen massacred in Algiers. A related inquiry (December, 1636) exposes another significant facet of the case: a request 'that the 2 Andaluzians may be delivered to ye English pilott, who was a principall cause of bringing in these Turks'. The '2 Andaluzians' could only have been small prize ships; again the determined avoidance of the pilot's name, together with the handsome award carefully not specified as such, confirm the impression that Dunton connived at his own capture. But this is one of the marvellous stories for which the Papers give no definite ending, so we never know whether the pirates were hanged or exchanged.

The Phantom Fleet

Of all the females openly or furtively present for centuries in Naval ships; of all the King's ships themselves in their crowding white-winged multitude of successive reigns; surely the most remarkable are the phantom women pictured below, sailing in phantom ships never seen on any ocean. The imagination that could project these visions must be allowed as impressive, seeing that its anonymous possessor was—by his own account—a common seaman heir to the common miseries of his class, unrelieved poverty and hardship.

The two distinct sections of this man's strange offering to

Charles I in February, 1636, which he calls his New Year's Gift, match in their duality the two distinct aspects of himself; one a typical Puritan of the repellent brimstone type, the other a husband and father groaning aloud at the plight of his family— yet by some peculiarly English miracle spurning all submissions of the spirit and retaining always the spark of courage and resource that burns, invincible if unrewarded, in his petition.

THE SEAMAN'S NEW YEAR'S GUIFT TO THE KING[1]

Most Royall king, this is my poor New Year's Guift.

English prisoners now in captivity to the Turks, are greater affliction'd than even Paules and Josephes.

O that it might stand with the good liking of your Majestie, that the whoares, harlotts and idle lascivious feamale sortt, the vomitte from the gutters, whom the lawe of God nor the lawes of your dominions, can nor will reclaime from their wilful lyfe ——

He now explains how the Harlotts, though impervious to reform, might be used for the benefit of the captives:

All might be changed; the lustfull desires of the heathen Turks might be fulfill'd; many intolerable crimes against Christians might be remedied; one harlott may prove to redeeme Captives; and by this [scheme] all may have their desires.

This universal beatitude may be achieved, he tells us, by his plan for exchanging 'one Harlott for halfe a dozen Englishmen'; the Heathen Turk, he feels, is sure to jump at such a bargain. When the barter has been arranged between the two countries, the Fleets are to be loaded with Whoares—but not ordinary Whoares; these girls will have been in special training, 'that they may deale with the Heathen, as Jaell with Sisera'. Having first made love to the Turks till they lapse into sated slumber, they will drive nails into their heads thus avenging the sufferings of their countrymen, then return triumphantly—by some means not stated—to England. 'And so may these branches spring to advance

[1] SP16/311/9

GOD'S GLORY,' the Seaman intones like Miriam, 'and spread your Majesties ensignes as a true defender of the FAITH'.

His Gift delivered, the Seaman begins without transition to speak from his heart, in his natural voice. *Wherein is the estate of the poore Sea-men Subiects of your Majestie to be lamented; who for want, are constrayned to leave their Wives and Families.* . . .

His plaint, like all such, is moving. But its effect seems completely overshadowed by the epic dimension of his first idea, standing alone in its grandeur: the concept of trollops recruited from docks, city pavements and stews by the shipload, indoctrinated with special techniques of brain-bashing instead of brain-washing, and marched into the King's ships to advance, under majestic full sail, against the Lustfull Turk.

Among the lost treasures of the Navy, haphazardly engulfed or cast up again by the element on which its drama was played, not the least is language; the mere English in which it speaks to us out of the Papers. From Lord High Admirals to the foulest-mouthed seaman in the pot-house come impacts of speech as untamed and ruthless as the seas that battered it into shape; a language whose unsparing force constantly brings the reader up short with pleasure, and as often with pain.

Of a blinded seaman, who today would call him 'a dark man'? What captain of today could match Francis Cranwell's mournful reproach to the Navy Officers: 'I see it is not ability but favour, which carries the game; old standards are left out who have borne the heat of day and cold of night, to cause y^r Honours to sleepe in peace?' Who today, in expressing a preference for a particular ship's doctor, could achieve the unconscious eloquence of Captain Mansell's, 'Hee knowes my bodie and my wound'?[1] The Earl of Sandwich relays a wicked tempest to the King: 'The weather grows Thicke; it Blows to that height of a Storme, that ye Sayles are blowne out of ye Bolt ropes.'[2]

The Earl's allusion to tempest winds and waves, conquered endless times but endlessly unconquered, reminds us of the chief

[1] SP29/98/98.   [2] SP29/132/83.

contenders in the immemorial struggle, the first-rate or line-of-battle ships. These, in their final development, became gigantic affairs requiring complements of seven hundred men and over, towering inert masses of tonnage having to be moved not by pressing buttons or tuning up diesels, but owing their least motion to the skill of the pygmies inside them. Yet these skills—perhaps at their topmost peak between 1790 and 1810, as displayed by the sea-captains called St Vincent's School—were such as to quicken the dead monster with the obedient, accurate and supple performance of a perfectly-trained horse; a sight probably wonderful beyond imagination, brought before us by Nelson's exultant shout from the deck of his ship, '*See* how that noble fellow Collingwood carries his ship into battle!'

Battles with enemy ships, however, could never compare in ferocity with that other battle, so often lost that sea-charts indicate where areas of the ocean floor are literally paved with wrecks. But marvellous to relate, there were men not impressed by force into the Navy, but who went out in Naval ships to face, of their own free will, the terrors of unequal combat with Nature again and again. The quality of these men, whom the terrors of mere enemy combat left unmoved, goes centuries farther back than Captain Plumleigh's undaunted voice that comes ringing to us across the dark trough of time, in a timeless Naval idiom: 'Above anie storme, my care hath prevayled.'[1]

[1] SP16/215.

INDEX